Last Frontiers For Mank

# Developing the
# MOUNTAINS

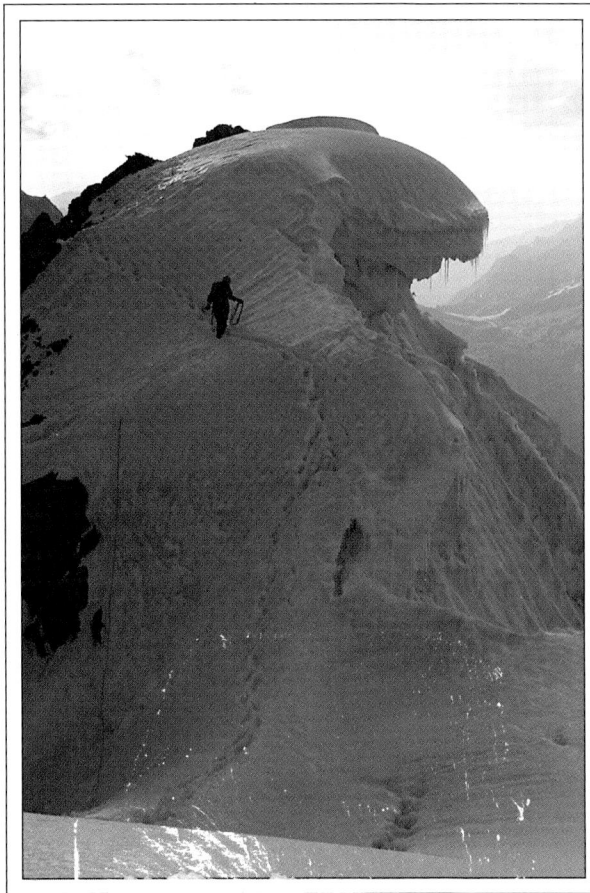

## Law          Williams

Evans                    ted

# CONTENTS

# INTRODUCTION

People have always been interested in mountains. Many people visit mountain lands for holidays. Some may be attracted by the scenery or by the chance to climb or ski. Others are attracted to study the rocks, the animals and the plants. Modern travel allows large numbers of people to reach almost all the mountainous places on Earth.

Mountains are important for many other reasons. They contain valuable minerals and building stones. They provide the opportunity to build dams and reservoirs. At many dams electricity is produced.

In some countries mountains are also very important for farming. Animals are grazed in the mountains in summer. In other countries, especially some tropical lands, steep slopes of mountains have been terraced to provide croplands. As populations increase so more mountain land will have to be turned into farm land. In some areas mountains are also important for their forests.

**Most ways of developing the mountains involve taking something out of the mountains rather than adding anything. The mountain lands are being exploited.** For example, minerals are mined, forests cut down, water pumped out. This is one reason why so many mountain lands are now in a state of crisis.

As the mountain lands continue to be exploited the crisis is getting worse. As the forests are cut down the soils are being washed away. As mining continues areas of great beauty are being permanently scarred.

This book is about the dangers involved in developing the mountains. It is also about what could be done to protect them.

**Walkers in the Flinders Range, South Australia.** Here a party of walkers can enjoy the mountains in the distance, the foothills in the foreground, and a wonderful display of wild flowers. One of the problems walkers cause is that they wear away footpaths. This can lead to soil erosion.

# CHAPTER ONE

# MOUNTAINS OF THE WORLD

The mountains of the world include many different environments. Compare the photograph on page 3 with the large cover photograph.

**One way of describing a mountain is by saying that it is high ground.** But what do we mean by high?

Mountains could be described as being more than 1000 metres (3280 feet) above sea level. In Great Britain this would mean there are no mountains in England. But in Wales there is Snowdon at 1085 metres (3559 feet), and in Scotland there is Ben Nevis at 1343 metres (4406 feet). But there is another problem as well. Large areas of the USA are above 1000 metres (3280 feet) but they are parts of the High Plains and are not mountains.

If we use a height of over 4000 metres (13 124 feet) above sea level then there are only two mountains in the whole of Western Europe: Mount Blanc (France) 4810 metres (15 780 feet), and the Matterhorn (Switzerland/Italy) 4477 metres (14 690 feet). At the 5000 metre (16 405 feet) limit there are no mountains at all in Western Europe. If the height limit used is 7500 metres (24 607 feet) the only mountains in the world are in the Himalaya and Karakoram Mountains in Asia.

There are other ways of describing mountains which do not refer just to height above sea level.

**Devil's Tower, Wyoming, USA**. This mountain is a good example of an almost flat-topped mountain with very steep sides. It is also a good example of an isolated peak separate from a mountain range. Compare this photograph with the one on page 5.

**The Kuh-I-Khuramij Mountains, Iran.** The size of these mountain ranges can be seen by comparing them with the trees and dried up river beds in the lower left-hand corner of the photograph. (Note how the mountain ranges form curved lines facing inwards. This is explained on page 16.)

For example:

1 **They are prominent features in the landscape.** They stand clear above the surrounding lowlands. (See the photograph above.)
2 **Most of them have areas of steep slopes.** This can be true even of mountains with nearly flat summits. (See the photograph on page 4.)

Mountains often occur in groups named mountain ranges. Most mountain ranges are long, narrow areas of very high ground. (See the map on page 6.) Large mountain ranges are not only high with steep slopes, they also have their own climates, plant life and animal life.

Mountains discussed in this book are high lands above sea level. But the ocean floors also have very high mountains. Some of these stand so high they reach the surface of the oceans as islands. The positions of some of the biggest **submarine mountain ranges** are shown in the map on page 6.

**Key words**

**crisis** – a time of change, a time of danger and opportunity.

**environment** – what a place is like and how the people live in it.

**exploited** – an environment from which something is taken out but nothing is added.

**foothills** – hills which lie at the edge of mountains. Foothills are lower than mountains. (See photograph on page 3.)

**isolated** – standing alone, not part of a group or range of mountains.

**landscape** – the scenery, what a place looks like.

**submarine** – under the sea.

**summit** – top or peak.

**tropical** – on or between the tropics of Cancer and Capricorn. (See the map on page 6.)

# LOCATION OF MOUNTAINS

Mountains can be described as areas of high ground which stand above the surrounding lowlands. Most mountains have some areas of steep slopes. Mountains often occur in groups named mountain ranges.

The map shows the location of the main mountain areas of the world. Because mountains are so different from each other they are difficult to show on a map. For example a mountain may be a hill that the local people want to name as a mountain. If a Sherpa from the Himalaya was taken to the top of Snowdon in Wales, and told he had just climbed a mountain, he would probably fall off the top from laughing so much. (The Welsh would not think this is funny.)

**This is how the map was drawn.**

1 **To show the location of important mountain ranges which are not very high,** all land between 1000 metres and 2000 metres (3280 and 6560 feet) has been coloured pale orange. As a result, the map shows mountain ranges such as the Appalachian Mountains in eastern North America, the Highlands of Scotland and the Flinders Range in Australia.

   The disadvantage of doing this is that many high plains areas are also shaded. Examples include central North America, much of South Africa.

2 **To show the major mountain ranges of the world** land between 2000 metres (6560 feet) and 4000 metres (13 124 feet) above sea level is coloured light brown. For example, this shows that the Rocky Mountains are bigger and higher ranges than the Appalachians in North America. In South America the Andes ranges are shown as much bigger and higher than the Brazilian Highlands.

3 **To show the location of the very highest mountain ranges of all** land more than 4000 metres (13 124 feet) above sea level is coloured dark brown. Most of this mountain land is in Asia and in South America. There are a few isolated peaks

above 4000 metres (13 124 feet) in Europe, Africa and North America.

In the oceans of the world two colours are used: blue and white. White shows the location of sea areas less than 4000 metres (13 124 feet) deep. As you would expect most of these areas are next to the continents. But some are not. They stretch into the middle of the oceans. These areas are where some of the submarine mountains ranges are found. The highest peaks here form islands. A few of them have been named on the map. This pattern is very clear on the mid-Atlantic Ridge and in the middle of the Indian Ocean.

MOUNTAINS OF THE WORLD

| Ocean depth in metres | Land height in metres |
|---|---|
| | 4000 |
| | 2000 |
| | 1000 |
| sea level | 0 |
| 4000 | |

Inland seas and lakes

# MOUNTAINS OF THE WORLD

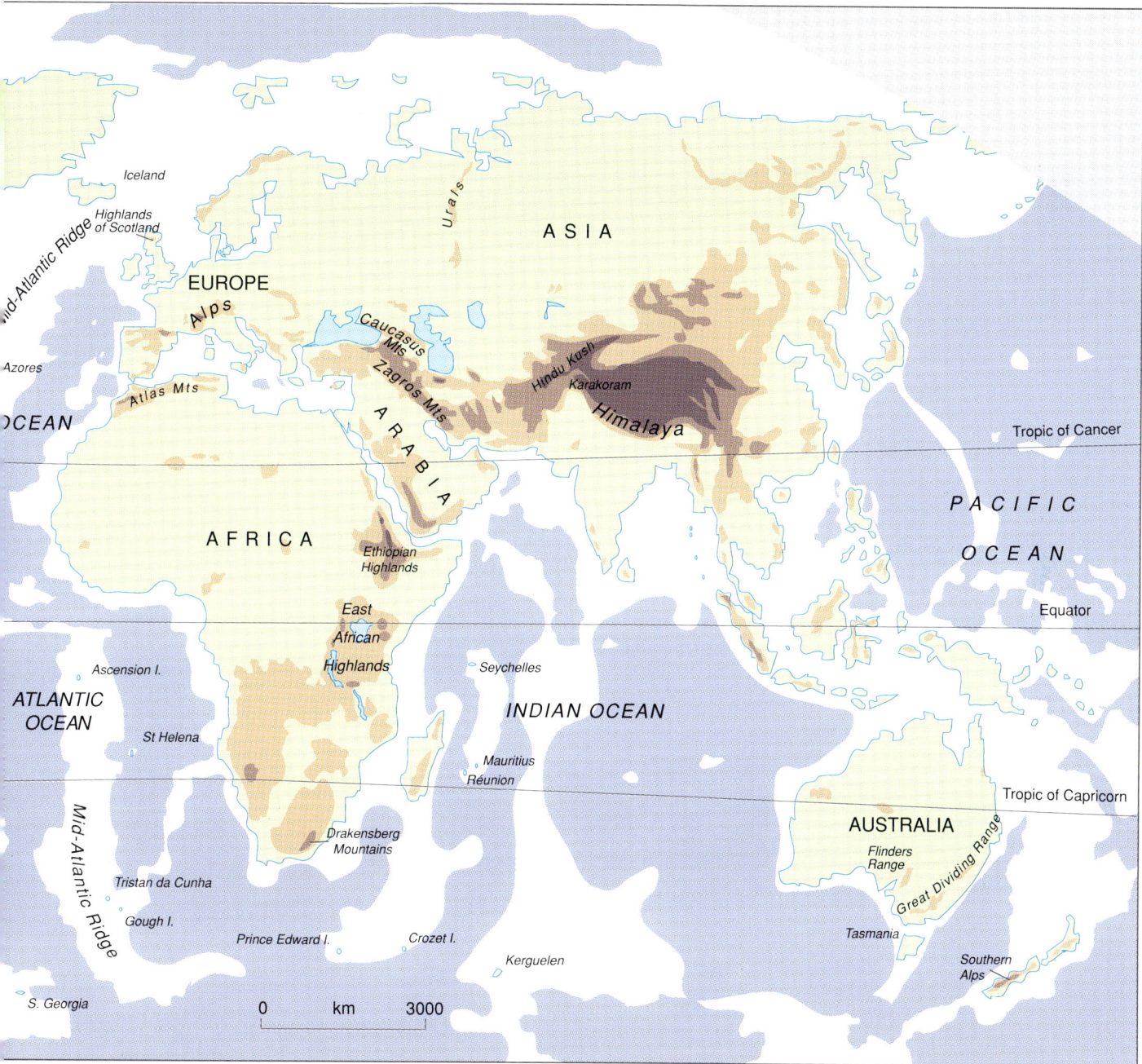

Iceland

Highlands of Scotland

Mid-Atlantic Ridge

ASIA

Urals

EUROPE

Alps

Azores

Caucasus Mts

Zagros Mts

Hindu Kush

Karakoram

Himalaya

Atlas Mts

OCEAN

ARABIA

Tropic of Cancer

PACIFIC

OCEAN

AFRICA

Ethiopian Highlands

East African Highlands

Seychelles

Equator

Ascension I.

ATLANTIC OCEAN

St Helena

INDIAN OCEAN

Mauritius

Réunion

Tropic of Capricorn

AUSTRALIA

Flinders Range

Great Dividing Range

Drakensberg Mountains

Mid-Atlantic Ridge

Tristan da Cunha

Gough I.

Prince Edward I.

Crozet I.

Tasmania

Southern Alps

Kerguelen

S. Georgia

0      km      3000

1 Draw freehand sketch maps of some of the mountain ranges shown in this map. In what ways are your maps alike?

2 In what ways are the land mountain ranges and the submarine mountain ranges alike?

3 Choose the largest map of North America in your atlas. Draw your own map of all the mountain ranges. Why is your map so different from the map of North America on this page?

**Key words**

**continent** – a very large land mass, e.g. Australia, South America.
**highlands** – often used to mean mountains, e.g. the Highlands of Scotland.
**island** – a small land area surrounded by water, e.g. Tasmania is an island but Australia is a continent.
**ocean** – a very large body of water covering a major part of the Earth's surface, e.g. the Pacific Ocean.

# CHAPTER TWO

# THE MAKING OF MOUNTAINS

## CONTINENTAL DRIFT

Mountains are made where the crust of the Earth is disturbed. The proof of this disturbance can be seen in the rocks. They are folded or faulted. (See the photographs on pages 5 and 16.) Today, we experience this disturbance happening through earthquakes and volcanic activity. (See the photographs on pages 12 and 13.)

**The main cause of mountain building is Continental Drift.** (See the diagram below.) The continents of the Earth rest upon enormous plates of rocks. These plates are very slowly moved about by currents in the hot molten layers underneath. The amount of movement may only be a few centimetres in a hundred years, but it has been happening for millions of years.

**When plates move together in a collision zone rocks are folded.** Molten rock, named magma, may be forced to the surface forming volcanoes. Great pressure may build up in these collision zones until the rocks suddenly move or break. The breaks are named faults. The shock waves of these sudden movements are named earthquakes.

An example of a modern collision zone is the Andes Mountains in South America. Here the Nazca Plate is in collision with the South American Plate. (See the diagram below and the map on page 11.)

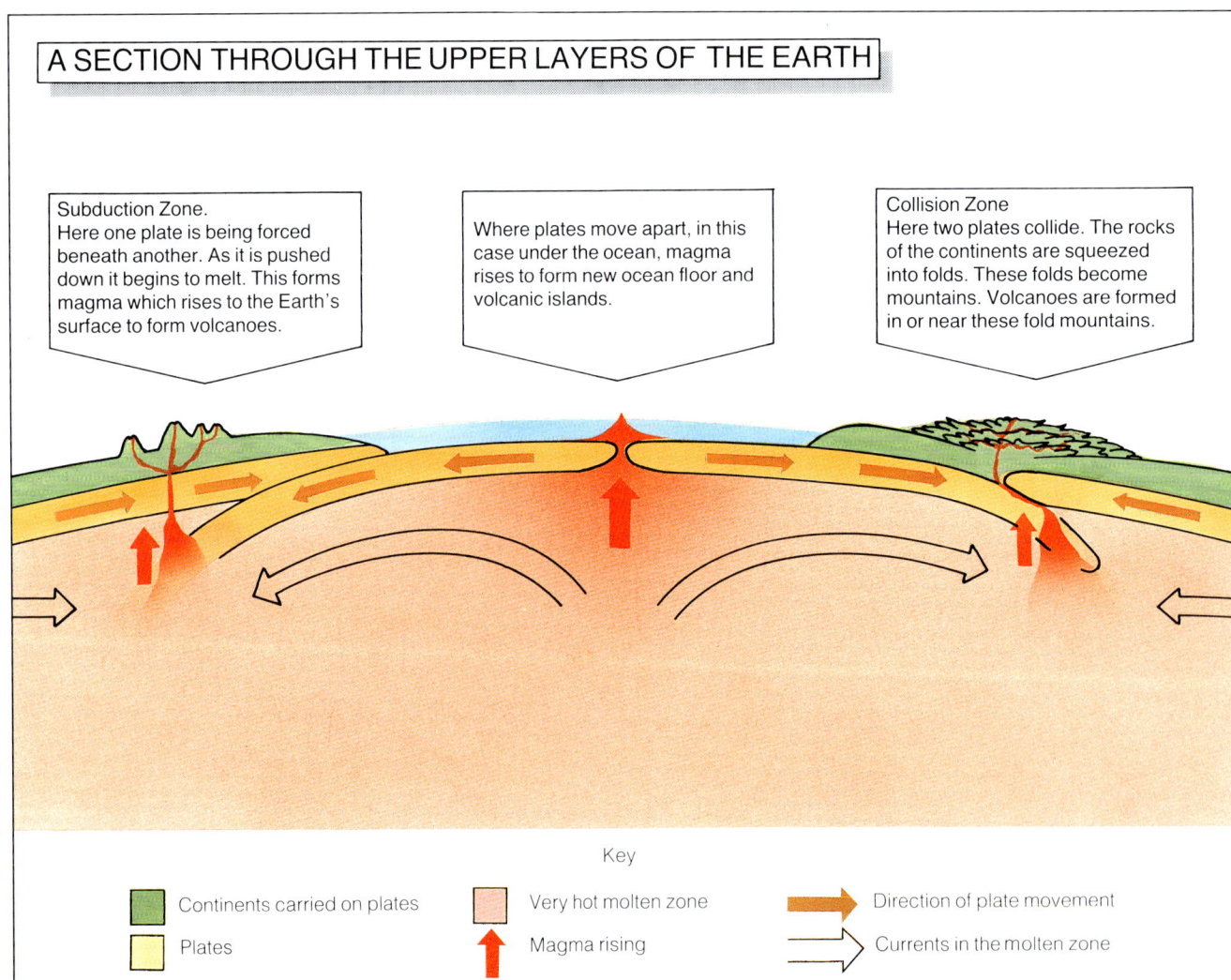

### A SECTION THROUGH THE UPPER LAYERS OF THE EARTH

Subduction Zone.
Here one plate is being forced beneath another. As it is pushed down it begins to melt. This forms magma which rises to the Earth's surface to form volcanoes.

Where plates move apart, in this case under the ocean, magma rises to form new ocean floor and volcanic islands.

Collision Zone
Here two plates collide. The rocks of the continents are squeezed into folds. These folds become mountains. Volcanoes are formed in or near these fold mountains.

Key

Continents carried on plates

Plates

Very hot molten zone

Magma rising

Direction of plate movement

Currents in the molten zone

## CONTINENTAL DRIFT IN THE LAST 200 MILLION YEARS

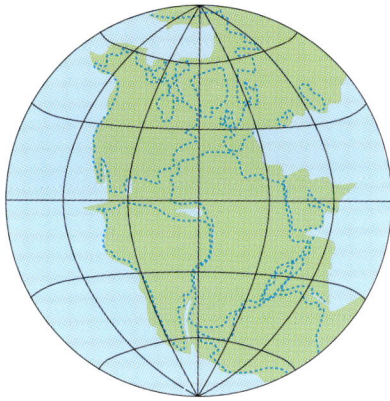

---------- Present day coastline

**200 million years ago**
The modern continents formed one enormous continent named Pangaea. Note that the continents fit at the edge of the continental shelf and not at the coastlines.

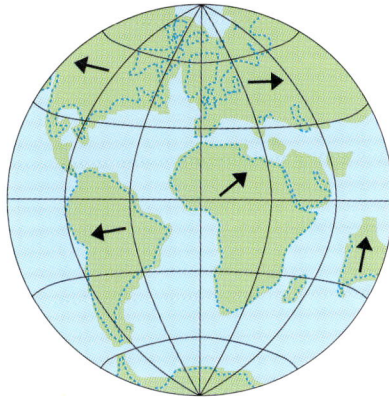

**60 million years ago**
The Atlantic Ocean is opening up. Note that India has moved north. Australia has moved east and round to the other side of the globe.

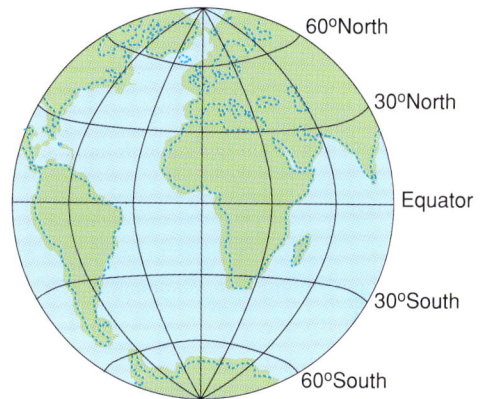

60°North
30°North
Equator
30°South
60°South

**Present Day**
Africa has moved north towards Europe. India has joined Asia. The Atlantic Ocean is fully open.

**In some other parts of the Earth plates are moving apart.** Here the cracks that open up in the crust allow magma to reach the surface and form new rocks. This often happens under the sea, and submarine volcanoes may result. The mid-Atlantic Ridge is a good example of new rocks forming where plates are moving apart. (See the diagram on page 8 and map on page 11.)

**Volcano erupting at Heimaey, Vestmanney, Iceland.** Iceland, and islands off the coast, are situated on the mid-Atlantic Ridge where there is much volcanic activity. Note that volcanic ash has not been cleared from all the roofs.

**Taulliraju Mountain, 5830 metres (19 129 feet) the Andes, Peru.**

The present-day movement of the plates began about 200 million years ago. (See the diagram on page 9.) This is very recent compared with the age of the Earth which is about 4600 million years. Geologists refer to all the newer fold mountains and volcanoes as young mountains. Even the mighty Himalaya are young mountains in geological time.

The older mountains of the Earth were also formed by Continental Drift. In those times the continents were moving in different directions from the ways they are moving now. For example, the Appalachian Mountains in eastern North America, the mountains of Wales, the Highlands of Scotland and the mountains of Norway were once all connected. They were formed about 400 million years ago when the North American Plate and the Eurasian Plate were moving towards each other. That was the opposite to the present-day movement.

**The eruption of Mount St Helens, Washington State, USA.** This was one of the most powerful eruptions in North America this century. Within a week volcanic ash and dust were detected above almost every country in the northern half of the Earth.

**Winter sunset at Hopi Point, Grand Canyon, Arizona, USA.** This view shows none of the violent activity of the other photograph on this page. But the power of mountain building is just as great here. These rocks have very gradually been raised to heights of nearly 2000 metres (6560 feet) above sea level.

# THE MAKING OF MOUNTAINS

## CONTINENTAL DRIFT TODAY

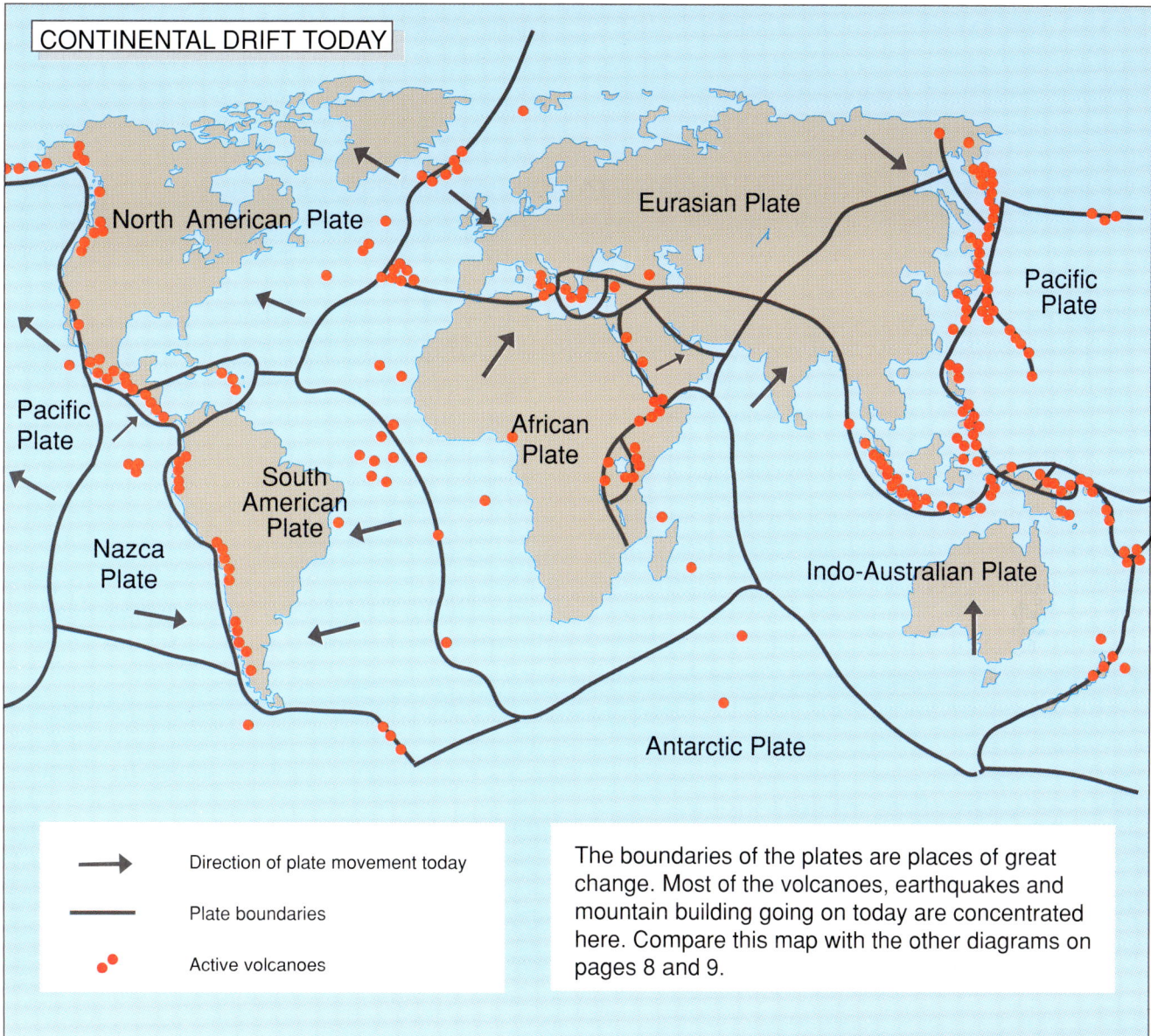

North American Plate

Eurasian Plate

Pacific Plate

Pacific Plate

African Plate

South American Plate

Nazca Plate

Indo-Australian Plate

Antarctic Plate

→ Direction of plate movement today

— Plate boundaries

•• Active volcanoes

The boundaries of the plates are places of great change. Most of the volcanoes, earthquakes and mountain building going on today are concentrated here. Compare this map with the other diagrams on pages 8 and 9.

**Key words**

**Continental Drift** – the very slow movement of the continents carried on plates. The plates are moved by slow currents in the hot molten layer under them.

**fault** – a break in the rocks.

**fold** – a bend in the rocks.

**magma** – hot molten rock in the interior of the Earth.

**volcanic activity** – the escape of magma, gases and steam to the Earth's surface. Mountains built by this process are named volcanoes.

1 Compare the map on this page with the map on page 6. What features on the continents follow the lines of the plate edges? What features in the oceans follow the line of the plate edges?

2 In the diagram on page 9, Iceland appears only on the world map for the present day. Why is this? (Looking at the map on this page will give a clue.)

3 As Continental Drift continues into the future what may happen to the Mediterranean Sea, the Red Sea, and to the East Indies? (Check the location of these places in your atlas.)

# VOLCANOES

Volcanoes play an important part in mountain building. The positions of some of the largest active volcanoes are shown in the map on page 11. Most of them are found near the plate edges. There are about 600 active volcanoes and every year about 50 of them erupt.

Volcanoes are of three types:
1 live and active
2 live and dormant (dormant means sleeping)
3 dead.

These names are used **in relation to geological time**. For example, the great volcano that once stood where Edinburgh in Scotland now stands, is dead. It has not erupted for 325 million years. (See page 15.)

Volcanoes that have not erupted in **historical time**, say the last 10 000 years, should not be named dead but regarded as dormant. For example, twelve of the fourteen most violent eruptions since the year AD 1800 have been **the first eruptions** at those places in historical time. History had suggested thay were dead when in fact they were dormant.

Dormant volcanoes are the most dangerous. There are two reasons for this:
1 Dormant volcanoes may have their cones sealed up by old lava. If they erupt again pressure may build up inside the cone. The eruption will begin with a very violent explosion. The whole top of the mountain may be blown off doing enormous damage.
2 Because dormant volcanoes may have been quiet for a long time many people may now live close to them. Their lives are at risk.

The most famous example of a dormant volcano coming to life unexpectedly is Mount Vesuvius in Italy. In AD 79 the volcano exploded. The towns of Pompeii and Herculaneum were buried, and most of the populations suffocated in the cloud of dust and ash. If this happens again many more people will die because so many Italians now live round the Bay of Naples. They believe the volcano is now harmless, but that was what the inhabitants of Pompeii believed.

**The crater of the Aso Volcano, Kyushu Island, Japan.** This is an active volcano that was fairly quiet at the time the photograph was taken. Steam is coming from the vent. At some other times this volcano was violently active and blew out this huge crater. At another time it poured out layers of lava which cooled to form solid rock. These layers can be seen on the right of the photograph. Many volcanoes show this changing pattern of eruptions.

## SOME DIFFERENT TYPES OF VOLCANOES

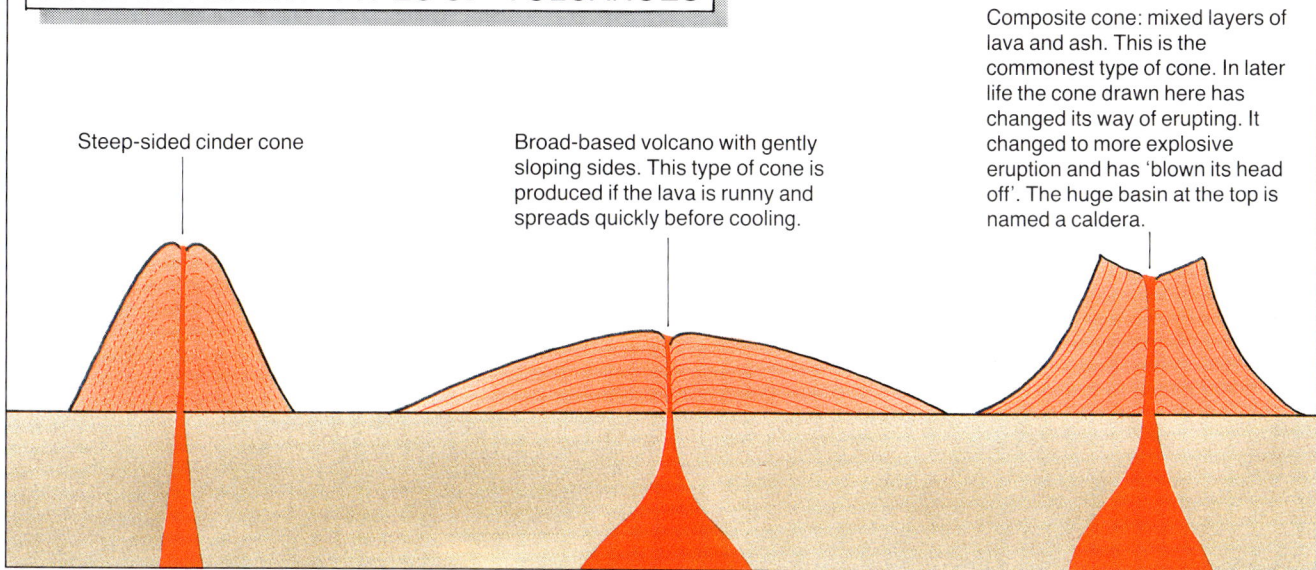

Steep-sided cinder cone

Broad-based volcano with gently sloping sides. This type of cone is produced if the lava is runny and spreads quickly before cooling.

Composite cone: mixed layers of lava and ash. This is the commonest type of cone. In later life the cone drawn here has changed its way of erupting. It changed to more explosive eruption and has 'blown its head off'. The huge basin at the top is named a caldera.

The situation today is that about 350 million people live near volcanoes that are either active or dormant. To make matters worse the 1980s have seen the biggest volcanic eruptions this century. These include Mount St Helens, North America (60 dead), El Chichon, Mexico (2000 dead) and Nevado del Ruiz, Columbia (22 000 dead).

The kinds of scenery formed by volcanoes depends on many different things. (See diagram above.) Two of the most important are:

1 the kind of material produced from the magma e.g. an ash cone, will be a different shape from a lava cone. A runny lava will build up a different kind of mountain to a stiff, slow-spreading lava.

2 the kind of hole (vent) by which the lava escapes.

**A Fire Fountain inside Stromboli, Italy.** Much of the material thrown out is ash and cinder.

**Key words**

**cone** – a collection of erupted material round a vent. The material may be built up into a hill or mountain named a volcano.

**dormant** – a volcano which is not erupting at the present time but which is not dead.

**eruption** – an escape of hot materials through a vent.

**geological time** – a very long time scale starting with the formation of the Earth 4600 million years ago.

**vent** – a hole through which lavas, ash, gases and steam escape to the Earth's surface.

NB. In the modern classification of volcanoes the word extinct is no longer used.

# DOME AND BLOCK MOUNTAINS

Where plates come together in Continental Drift, rocks may be disturbed by rising magma or they may break. In these places dome mountains or block mountains are produced. Some examples are shown in the diagram below.

Two examples of dome mountains are the Lake District in England, and the Black Hills of Dakota in the USA. As the diagram shows the rising magma does not reach the surface through volcanoes. Instead it causes the rocks above it to dome upwards. The magma cools slowly to form rocks very different from the rapidly cooled lavas in volcanoes.

When rocks are placed under great pressure they may either fold or break. Breaks in rocks are named faults. Many faults are quite small. An example is shown in the diagram below.

Faults can also be extremely large. They may run for many hundreds of kilometres across country and have great effects on the scenery. If a block of the crust slips down between faults it forms a rift valley. (See the diagram below.) One of the largest rift valleys is occupied by the Red Sea. It is bordered by the block mountains of Arabia on the east side, and by the block mountains of north-east Africa on the west side. The position of this rift valley at the meeting of two plates is shown in the map on page 11. Further south lies another great rift valley: the East Africa Rift Valley.

In North America a huge area of the USA, between the Rocky Mountains and the Coast Ranges, is made of block mountains. This is known as the Basin and Range region of the USA. Part of it borders the area of the Grand Canyon. (See the photograph on page 10.) In this area the rocks show little sign of folding. Rocks have been faulted and then raised, lowered or tilted.

In some parts of the world today some faults are very unstable. There is a lot of movement, frequent earthquakes, and sometimes volcanic activity at the same time. The best known example is the San Andreas Fault in the western USA. This runs parallel to the west coast through much of California. Unfortunately, this part of the USA is a very attractive place in which to live. Many millions of people live on or near the fault. Some scientists suggest there will be a terrible disaster here in the next few years, and that it may be far worse than the San Francisco Earthquake in 1906.

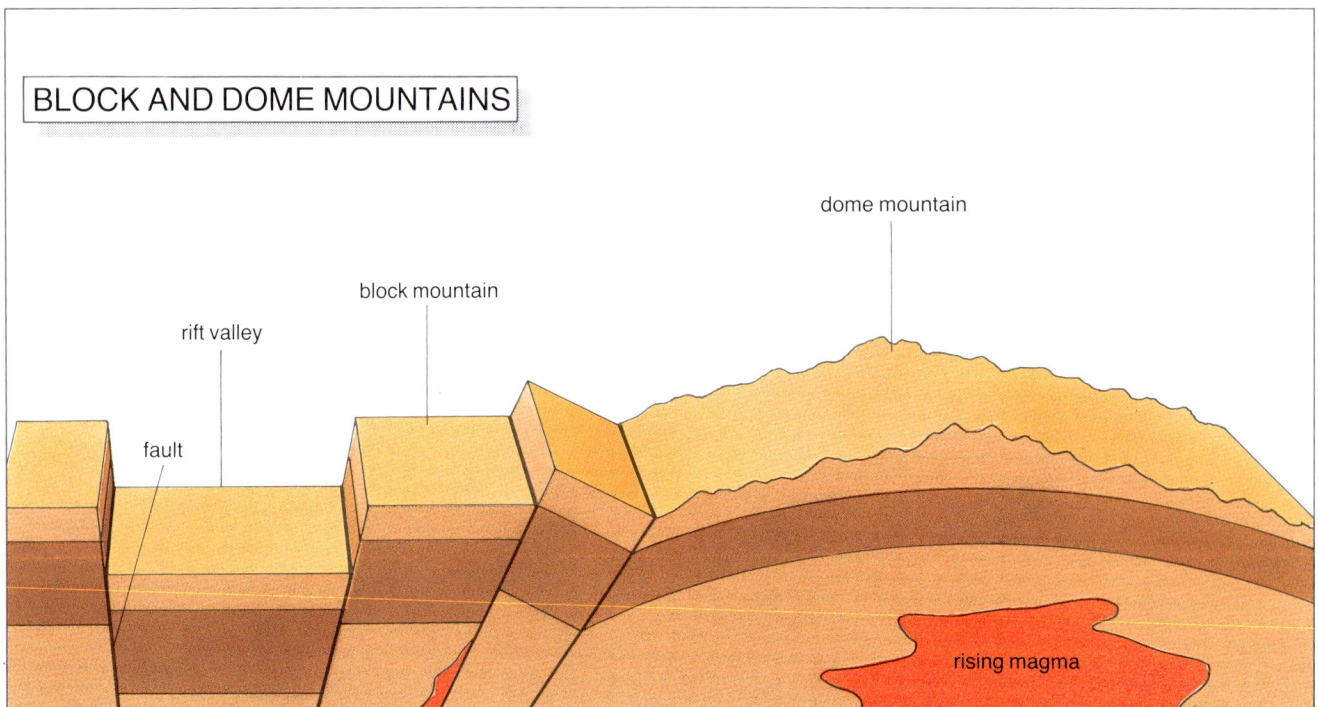

BLOCK AND DOME MOUNTAINS

rift valley

block mountain

dome mountain

fault

rising magma

## EROSION OF A VOLCANO AT EDINBURGH, SCOTLAND

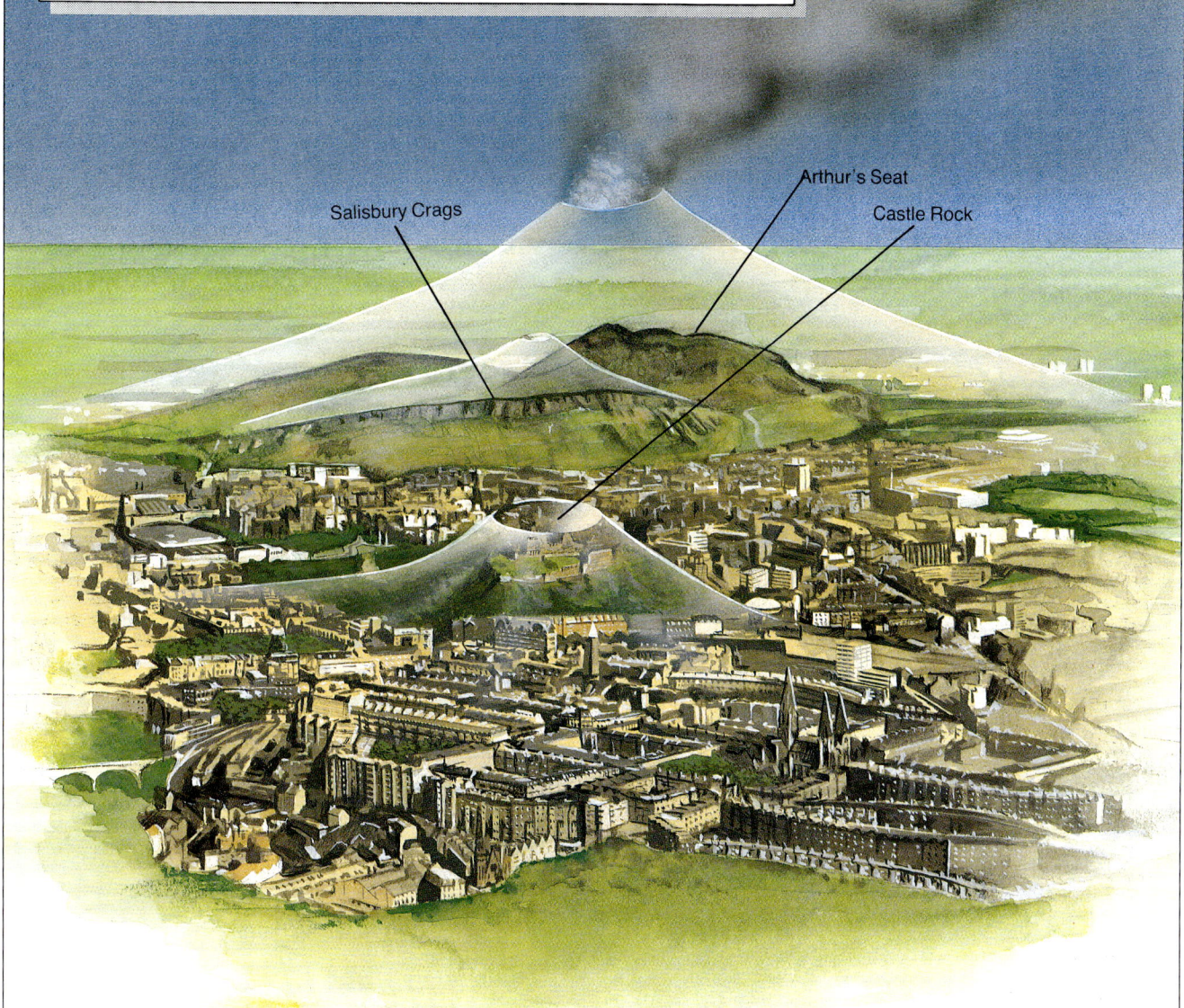

Salisbury Crags

Arthur's Seat

Castle Rock

This diagram shows that Edinburgh is built on the site of a dead volcano (see page 12). The volcano was last active about 325 million years ago. The volcano had a large main cone, and some smaller cones on its sides. The volcano has been drawn in on this picture of Edinburgh.

The main cone has been worn away until only the hills, named Arthur's Seat, remain. One of the smaller cones has been worn down in the middle distance to form Salisbury Crags. The stump of another small cone forms Castle Rock, Edinburgh, in the foreground.

The dead volcano is the structure on which Central Edinburgh now stands. This **structure** has been **eroded** by the **process** of seas, rivers and glaciers. This has been happening for a **time** of 325 million years (see page 18).

# FOLD MOUNTAINS

When horizontal rocks are squeezed from the side they may develop **folds**. This is shown in the diagram below.

Simple folds with roughly equal folding on each side are named anticlines and synclines. The photograph on page 5 shows an anticline broken open by erosion. If a fold is dipping more steeply on one side than the other it is named an asymmetrical fold. If folding is severe the folds may lay on top of each other. These are named recumbent folds. Lastly, under very severe pressure, folds may be torn from their roots along fault lines. These are the nappe folds at the right-hand end of the diagram.

Folds can be very small or they can be several kilometres across. The photograph on the right shows small folds in rocks in Norway. The **dip** of the folds can be compared with the horizontal line of the skyline.

The top photograph on page 17 shows much bigger folds on a shoulder of a mountain in the Austrian Alps.

The rocks involved in folding are nearly all **sedimentary** rocks. They were **deposited** on a sea floor. Trapped within them are the skeletons of many sea creatures. These we name fossils. These fossils allow us to work out the ages of the rocks, and the order they were deposited in the sea. (See the bottom photograph on page 17.)

Where great thicknesses of sedimentary

**An example of intense folding on the Norwegian coast.** This is a small example but includes many of the features found on a large scale in fold mountains.

rocks were folded by severe pressure, ranges of fold mountains were produced. For example, when India was far to the south of Asia, the sea floor between the continents was made of sedimentary rocks. When India moved towards Asia those rocks were squeezed by severe pressure and began to be folded. (See the diagram on page 9.) This folding continued over millions of years until the Himalaya and other young mountain ranges of Asia were formed. Even the rocks in the top of Mount Everest contain fossils of sea creatures.

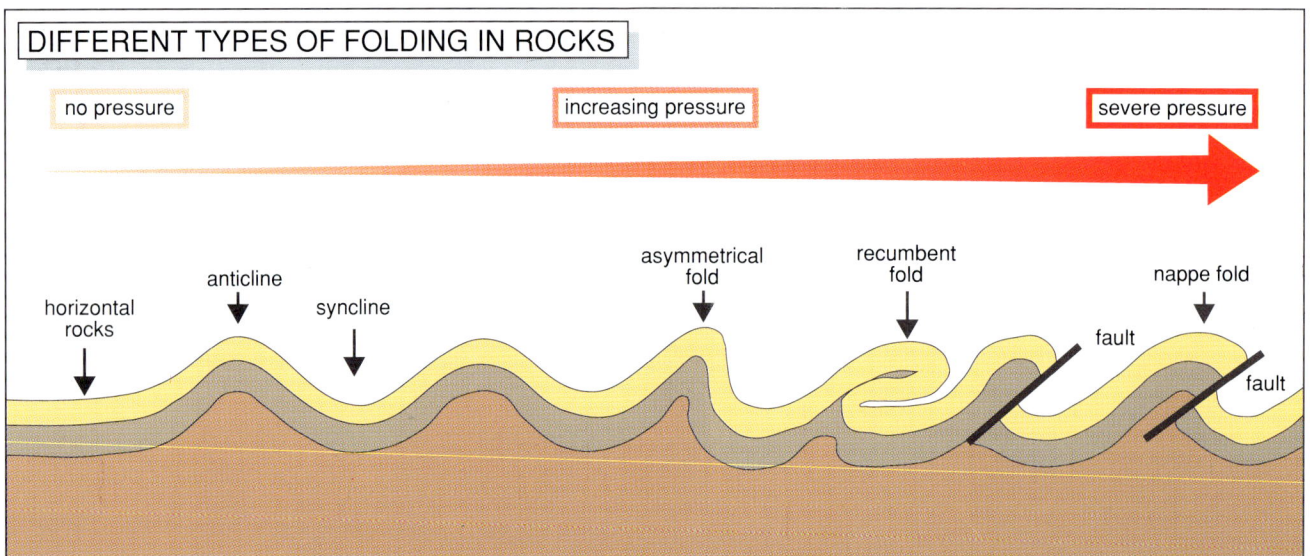

## DIFFERENT TYPES OF FOLDING IN ROCKS

no pressure · increasing pressure · severe pressure

horizontal rocks · anticline · syncline · asymmetrical fold · recumbent fold · nappe fold · fault · fault

**Folding in the Austrian Alps.** The bare shoulder of the mountain shows a clear pattern of folds.

**An example of fossils of marine creatures that lived in the seas 175 million years ago.** These are named ammonites.

**Key words**

**dip** – the angle at which rocks slope, Horizontal rocks have a dip of 0° Vertical rocks have a dip of 90°.
**deposited** – laid down.
**folds** – bends in rocks. Some key words about folds are explained on page 16.
**sedimentary** – rocks laid down in layers of sediment, usually in water. The muds, sands, etc. that form the rocks are carried into the seas or lakes by rivers, melt water from glaciers or by the wind and rain.

1  Place a table cloth or towel on a table. Using both hands push the opposite ends of the cloth towards each other. How many kinds of folds can you make?
2  Draw a larger version of the photograph on page 16: **Folding in Norway.** Label as many different types of folds as you can.

# MOUNTAIN SCENERY

The sort of mountain scenery found in a particular place depends on how the rocks are arranged, and what kinds of rocks they are. This is named **structure**. For example, if the structure is folded rocks the mountain scenery will be different from the scenery on volcanic rocks. (Compare the photograph on page 5 with the one on page 12.) Scenery on sandstone rocks is different from scenery on limestone rocks. (Compare the two photographs on page 19.)

Mountain scenery also depends on how the rocks are attacked by **erosion** and **weathering**. This is named **process**. Processes include attack by rain and rivers or attack by frost and ice (glaciation). Process often picks out weaknesses in rocks. Look again at the photograph on page 5. It shows how an anticline has been broken open leaving curved mountain ranges facing each other.

The third way mountain scenery is formed is decided by how long the processes have been working . This is the effect of **time**. For example, the volcanic scenery in the photograph on page 12 is quite different from the volcanic scenery in the drawing on page 15.

**The three main things that decide the kind of mountain scenery found in a particular place are structure, process and time.** The photographs on these pages show that climate and plants also play a part. (See chapter 3, page 20.)

**Key words**

**erosion** – the break-up and removal of rocks. An example is the break-up and removal of rocks by a glacier. (See the photographs below.)
**scenery** – what a place looks like.
**weathering** – the break-up of rocks by the weather, for example, the frost-shattering of rocks. This is shown in the large photograph on page 19. (The word erosion is used only if the rock pieces are carried away.)

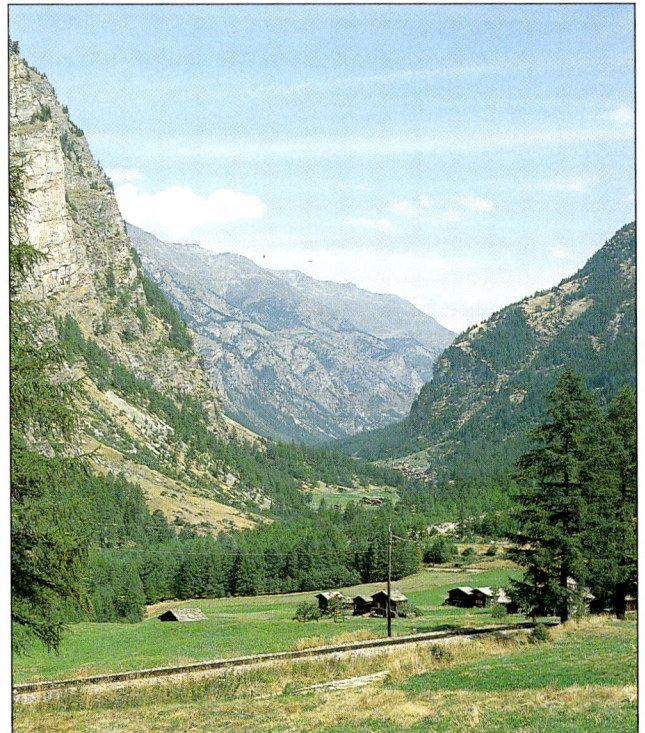

**Glaciated mountain scenery in Switzerland.** The left-hand photograph shows an area being glaciated now. The Monte Rosa mountains feed ice and rock pieces into the Gornier glacier. The glacier is in a deep U-shaped valley. The right-hand photograph, taken near Zermatt, shows an area glaciated in the past. The steep-sided U-shape of the valley is clearly shown.

**Different kinds of limestone scenery.** The main photograph shows three summits in the Italian Alps at almost 3000 metres (9843 feet) above sea level. The inset photograph is of a group of summits just below 1000 metres (3280 feet) in South China. Both groups of mountains are made mainly of limestone.

**Sandstone mountains in the desert near Tabul, Saudi Arabia.**

1 Look at the photographs on these pages. They all show mountain scenery with high peaks. What do they also show about **slopes** in mountain country?
2 The two photographs above **both** show mountainous limestone scenery. Suggest at least two reasons why they are so different. (Use the word **process** in part of your answer.)
3 Two photographs are of places with hot tropical climates. Which are they? Why is the mountain scenery so different in the two places?

# CHAPTER THREE

# WEATHER, PLANTS AND ANIMALS IN MOUNTAIN LANDS

## The Weather of the Mountain Lands

It is almost impossible to speak about mountain **climates** because conditions vary so much from place to place and hour to hour. **Average** temperature and rainfall figures mean very little.

There are two basic facts about mountain weather that apply in many places:
1  With increasing altitude there is increasing precipitation.
2  With increasing altitude there is decreasing temperature.

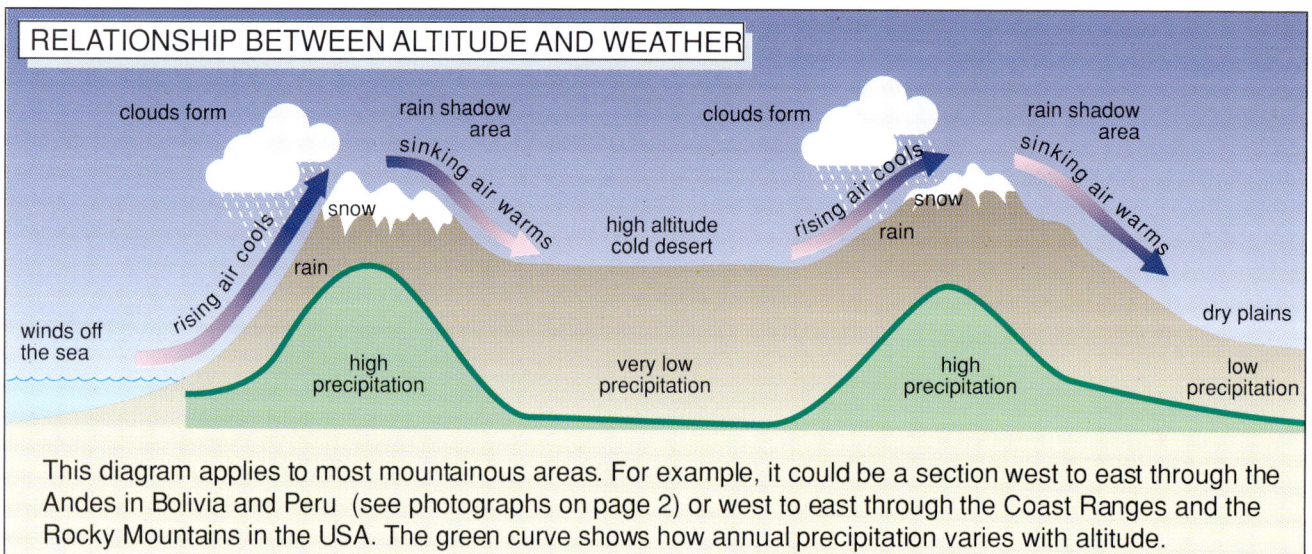

RELATIONSHIP BETWEEN ALTITUDE AND WEATHER

clouds form

rain shadow area

sinking air warms

clouds form

rain shadow area

sinking air warms

rising air cools

snow

high altitude cold desert

rising air cools

snow

rain

rain

winds off the sea

dry plains

high precipitation

very low precipitation

high precipitation

low precipitation

This diagram applies to most mountainous areas. For example, it could be a section west to east through the Andes in Bolivia and Peru (see photographs on page 2) or west to east through the Coast Ranges and the Rocky Mountains in the USA. The green curve shows how annual precipitation varies with altitude.

Mountains show other variations in weather apart from those explained by the effect of altitude. These include the effects of aspect and slope.

1 **Aspect**  Aspect means the direction in which a slope faces. A mountain slope facing toward the sun will have different weather from the shady slope. One result may be that farming is possible quite high up on the sunny side of a valley. The shady aspect side may be entirely covered with coniferous forest. (See the photograph on page 29.)

2 **Slope**  The steeper the slope the faster cold, heavy air will slide down it. This rapid movement of air may damage plants by drying them out. It may also damage crops by bringing very cold air into the valleys. Temperatures have been recorded showing a drop from 15°C to −1°C (59°F to 30°F) in two hours. If cold air moves downhill very quickly then strong winds develop. The winds are speeded up by the effect of gravity (katabatic winds). Speeds as high as 250 kilometres per hour (155 miles per hour) have been recorded.

The other important feature of mountain weather is that it varies from hour to hour as well as from place to place. Warm days can be followed by bitterly cold nights. Clear skies may cloud over in an hour or two. It is probably true that more mountaineers have been killed by sudden changes in the weather than by mistakes in climbing skills.

**This Yak lives in Nepal at an altitude of 4000 metres (13 124 feet).** It is a member of a herd kept by local people. The yak's very long thick coat helps it survive the intensely cold nights and winters at this altitude.

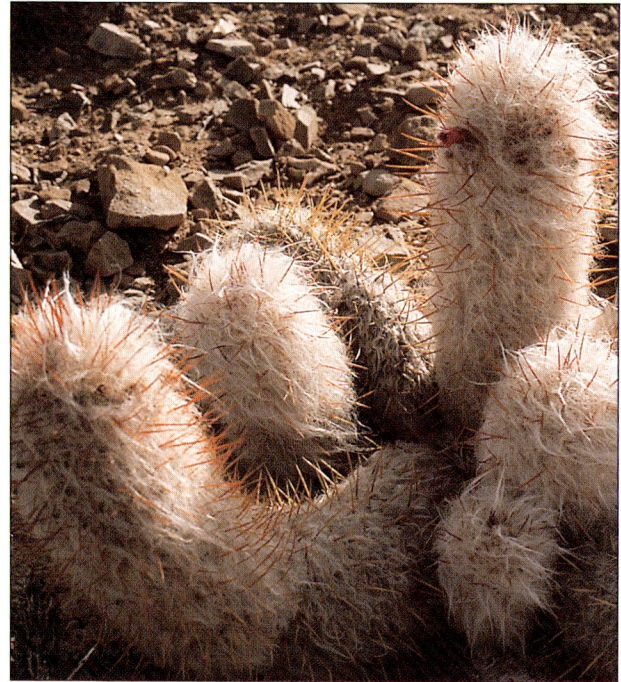

**Cactus at 4000 metres (13 124 feet) in the Andes, Bolivia.** This cactus is growing not in a hot desert but in a high altitude cold desert. Its cover of needle-like hairs protects it both from grazing animals and from the cold. Compare this photograph with the one on the left. Some animals and plants are protected from the cold in similar ways.

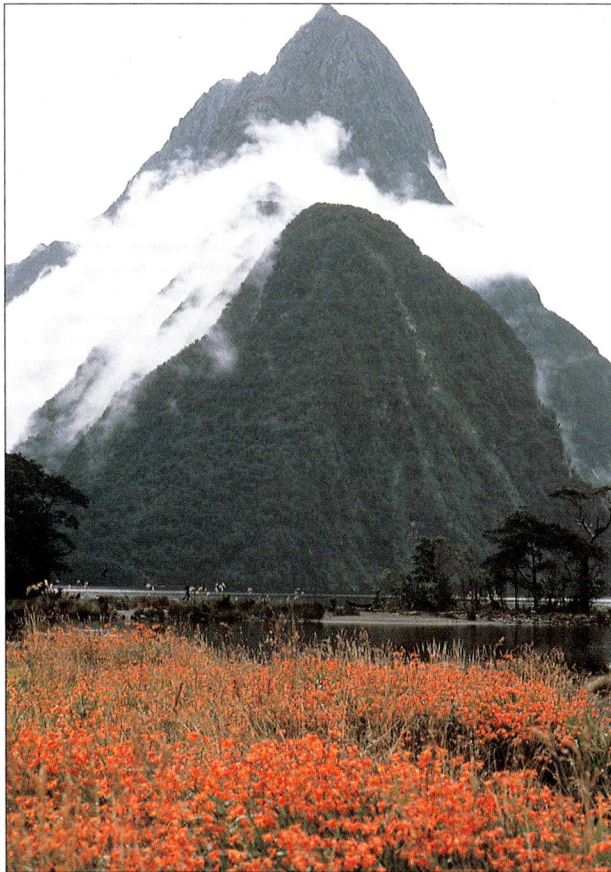

**A mountain scene in New Zealand.** Cold air approaching from the left is being forced to rise forming cloud. (Compare this with the diagram on page 20.) This picture also shows three zones in this mountain area. There is a bare rock summit, below it is a tree-covered shoulder and slopes, and below that a broad valley floor with trees and flowers. (See pages 22 and 23.)

### Key words

**average** – the result of adding up some figures and dividing the answer by the number of figures. For example, the average temperature of 30°C, 10°C and 5°C is 15°C. Note that the average temperature did not occur.

**climate** – average weather conditions over at least 35 years. In mountain lands the weather is so variable averages do not mean much.

**katabatic winds** – winds speeded up by the effect of gravity as they flow downhill.

**precipitation** – all the forms in which water falls onto the ground e.g. dew, fog, frost, hail, rain, and snow.

**weather** – local changes in conditions of temperature, precipitation etc. day by day or even hour by hour.

The plants and animals of the mountain lands are adapted to the conditions. But most of the conditions limit plant growth rather than encourage it.

The main difficulties facing plants and animals are:
1 Temperatures decrease with altitude.
2 High precipitation waterlogs the soils.
3 There is a large difference in temperatures between day and night.
4 Increased cloudiness reduces sunlight.
5 High winds dry out plant leaves.

In addition, the soils are often thin and infertile. They are easily eroded away on the slopes making it even more difficult for plants to grow and spread.

Plants that grow well are often adapted to a very short growing season. They can also survive the violent weather. Plants often have strong roots but short stems. Some have spiky leaves and others are covered with hair or spines that let in heat and light but reduce air movement. (See the photograph of the cactus on page 21 and of ichu grass on page 27.)

Many animals show adaptations similar to plants. They have thick, long coats that reduce air movement and keep out the cold.

A good example is the Yak. (See the photograph on page 21.) Yaks can survive to altitudes of 6000 metres (19 686 feet) in Nepal and Tibet. The members of the camel family, such as vicuna and llama (see the photographs on page 23 and on page 25) are also protected from the weather by their fine, wool coats. Other animals such as hares and marmots put on layers of fat in summer and hibernate or semi-hibernate in winter.

Vegetation is usually arranged in zones on mountains. The diagram below shows some of these zones for places at different distances from the Equator. Below the permanent snow is an area of Alpine meadow which is mainly grasses, wild flowers and small shrubs. Below the Alpine meadow zone the vegetation passes through a whole series of zones down to tropical evergreen forest near the Equator. Further north towards the Pole fewer and fewer zones are found until, inside the Arctic circle, permanent snow reaches to the sea.

In the southern half of the world similar zones are found but the types of trees are not quite the same. For example, in Australia, southern beech and eucalyptus trees are more important than conifers.

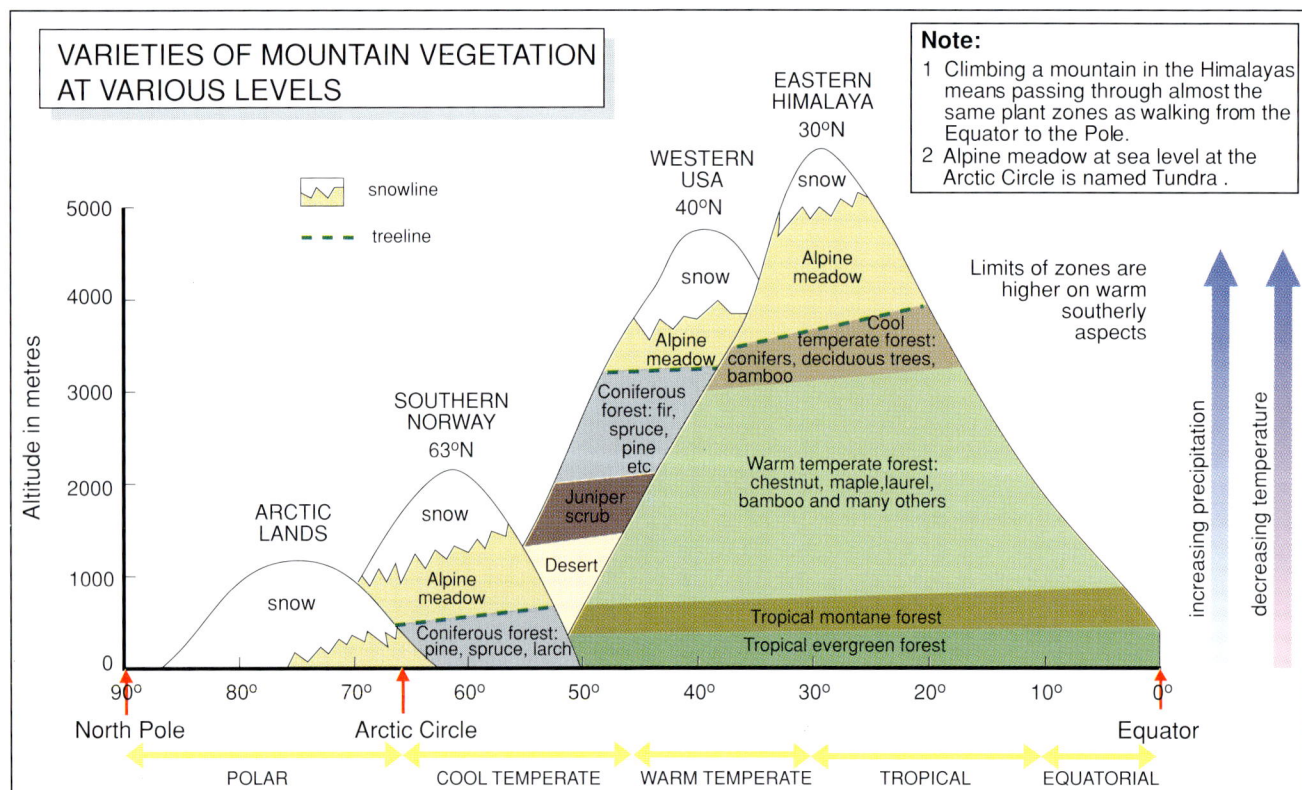

VARIETIES OF MOUNTAIN VEGETATION AT VARIOUS LEVELS

Note:
1 Climbing a mountain in the Himalayas means passing through almost the same plant zones as walking from the Equator to the Pole.
2 Alpine meadow at sea level at the Arctic Circle is named Tundra.

### Different vegetation zones on the same mountain

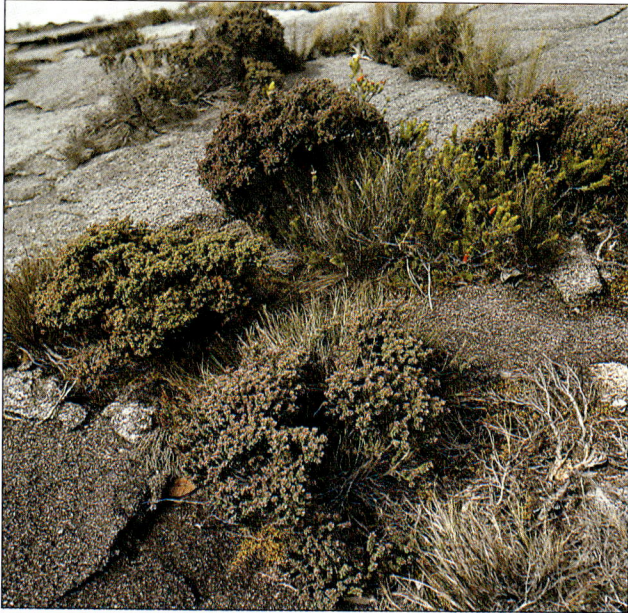

**Alpine Zone on Mount Kinabalu, Borneo.** Here are shrubs and tough grasses growing on the small amounts of soil remaining in the rock cracks. The rock itself is covered with lichens. Lichens are a group of plants that can grow without soil.

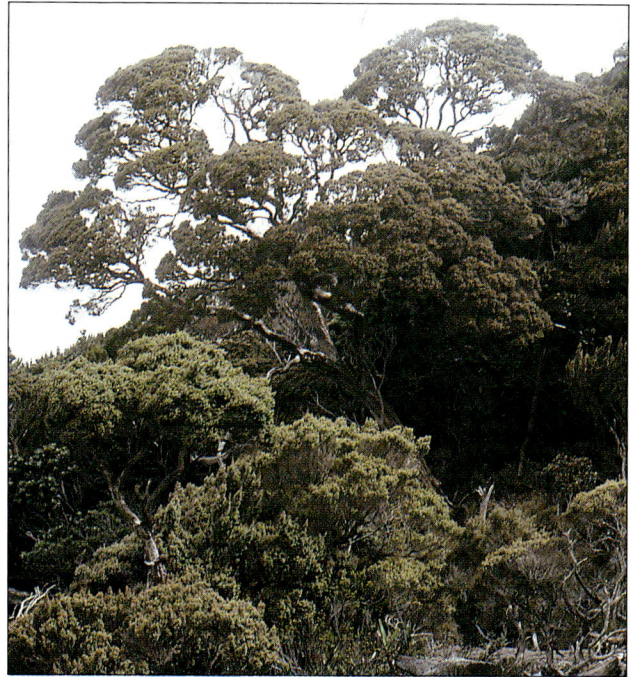

**Montane tropical forest on Mount Kinabalu, Borneo.** The trees here are near the tree line so they are low-growing. (In temperate lands there would be conifers at this altitude.)

**Llama herd in the Andes, Bolivia.** Although they belong to the camel family, llamas do not have humps. But they are easily recognized because of their long necks and thick coats. This herd is grazing on Alpine meadow. In the distance can be seen permanent snow on peaks rising to about 6000 metres (19 686 feet).

**Key words**

**adaptation** – an alteration that allows a plant or animal to survive in its environment.
**coniferous** – trees which carry cones, e.g. pine and fir. The leaves are usually evergreen needles.
**deciduous** – trees that drop their leaves in autumn (fall) e.g. oak and chestnut. (Very few trees are both coniferous **and** deciduous. One example is the larch.)
**montane** – on a mountain.

Look at all the photographs in this book and make a list of which mountain vegetation zones are shown in which pictures. Which mountain zone is shown most often?

# CHAPTER FOUR

# PEOPLE WHO LIVE IN THE MOUNTAINS

The first half of this book has shown that there are many kinds of mountain environments. How mountain peoples live in these environments also varies from place to place.

1 Very few people live in the mountains. Most of the Earth's population lives between sea level and an altitude (height) of 1000 metres (3280 feet).

2 In several mountain countries the mountain peoples are the poorest people. Compared with the people in the lowlands they have a poorer diet, are less well educated and earn less money. Even in wealthier mountain countries like Switzerland and Norway this difference is still found today.

There are several reasons why the mountain lands are so empty, and many of the people so poor.

1 **The high altitude**

Some mountain peoples live in places where the lower ground is between 3500 and 4500 metres (11 483 and 14 764 feet). This is higher than many of the mountain peaks in Europe. People from lowlands who come here suffer from breathlessness, dizziness and sickness. This is because there is so much less oxygen available at high altitude. But mountain dwellers, like the Sherpas of Nepal and the Quechua Indians of Peru, have slightly larger lungs and hearts than other people. They can live quite comfortably at these altitudes.

2 **Isolation**

Many mountain lands are far from the plains and the cities. Benefits such as electricity, modern medicine and good schooling have not reached some places.

3 **Mountain climates are harsh climates**

Winters are very cold. In all seasons night temperatures may be very low compared with the day. The weather is also very unreliable. (See page 20.)

4 **Steep slopes and lack of level land**

In many places crops can be grown only on terraces built on steep mountain sides. (See the small photograph on the cover and also page 25.)

5 **Lack of fertile soils**

Very few mountain areas have naturally fertile soils. When the land is terraced the soils have to be improved by adding animal and human manures.

**Shrines in the mountains, Ladakh, India.** Most peoples of the world have at some time regarded mountains as holy places. They have built temples and other shrines there. In addition to these shrines, or stupas, this photograph also shows the infertile and bare soils of this high ground.

**House and farmland in the Himalaya, Nepal.** This house is one of several in a village at about 1000 metres (3280 feet) above sea level. Houses are scattered because there is no single area of flat land where they can stand together. The villagers keep animals and also farm terraced slopes. The main crop is rice.

**Children from Manang Village, Annapurna Mountains, Himalaya, Nepal.** These children are used to living at 3500 metres (11 483 feet) above sea level.

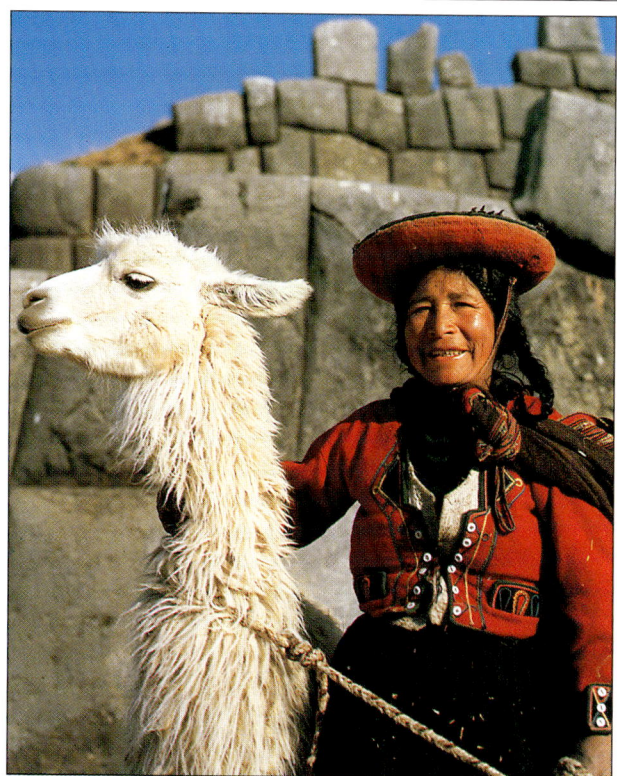

**Quechua Indian woman with llama, from Cuzco, Peru.** Both are happy to live at high altitude. (See page 26.)

# INDIANS OF THE ANDES

The largest surviving group of Indians in the Andes Mountains in South America is the Quechua people. They live in Ecuador, Peru and Bolivia. They are fortunate that their lands include several broad plains between the mountains. Although these plains are very bleak and stand at 3500 to 4000 metres (11 483 to 13 124 feet) above sea level, they include some areas suitable for farming. A second group of Indians, the Ayamara people, live around Lake Titicaca on the border between Bolivia and Peru.

These people were badly treated by the Spanish settlers in the 16th and 17th centuries. Later, they were ill-treated by their own governments that ruled them from the cities. But today they are developing their own modern way of life.

The photographs below, and the photograph of the Quechua woman on page 25, give some idea of their way of life now.

The majority of them are farmers. Their most important crops are barley and potatoes. They also keep cattle, sheep and poultry. Their diet is improved by fish from Lake Titicaca and mountain streams.

The Quechua Indians are famous for rearing and farming the llama and its relative the vicuna. These animals belong to the camel family but do not have humps. They are valued by the Indians as pack animals that can carry goods across the mountains. They are also valuable for their wool. Some of the wool is exported, some is woven into colourful textiles by the Indians themselves.

These Indian peoples were treated little better than slaves only 50 years ago. But they are now developing their way of life including the use of modern farming machinery and medicines.

One problem this is causing is that the population is beginning to increase quite rapidly. This is one reason why so many young Indians are leaving the countryside for towns like La Paz.

Indians are also moving to the towns and the tin mines in search of a higher standard of living. But this is creating another problem where towns are becoming overcrowded, and slum conditions are spreading.

**Indians fishing from their totora reed boats on Lake Titicaca.**

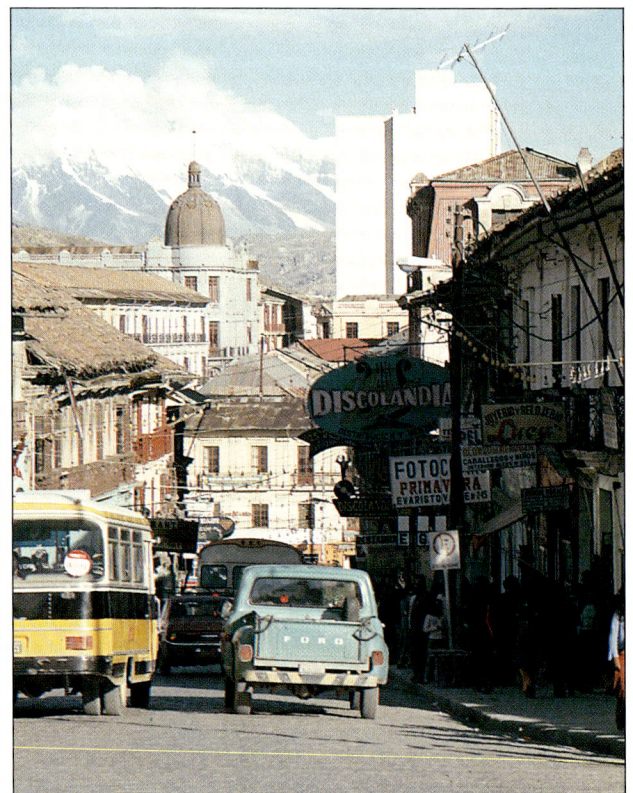

**A view in La Paz, mountain capital of Bolivia.**

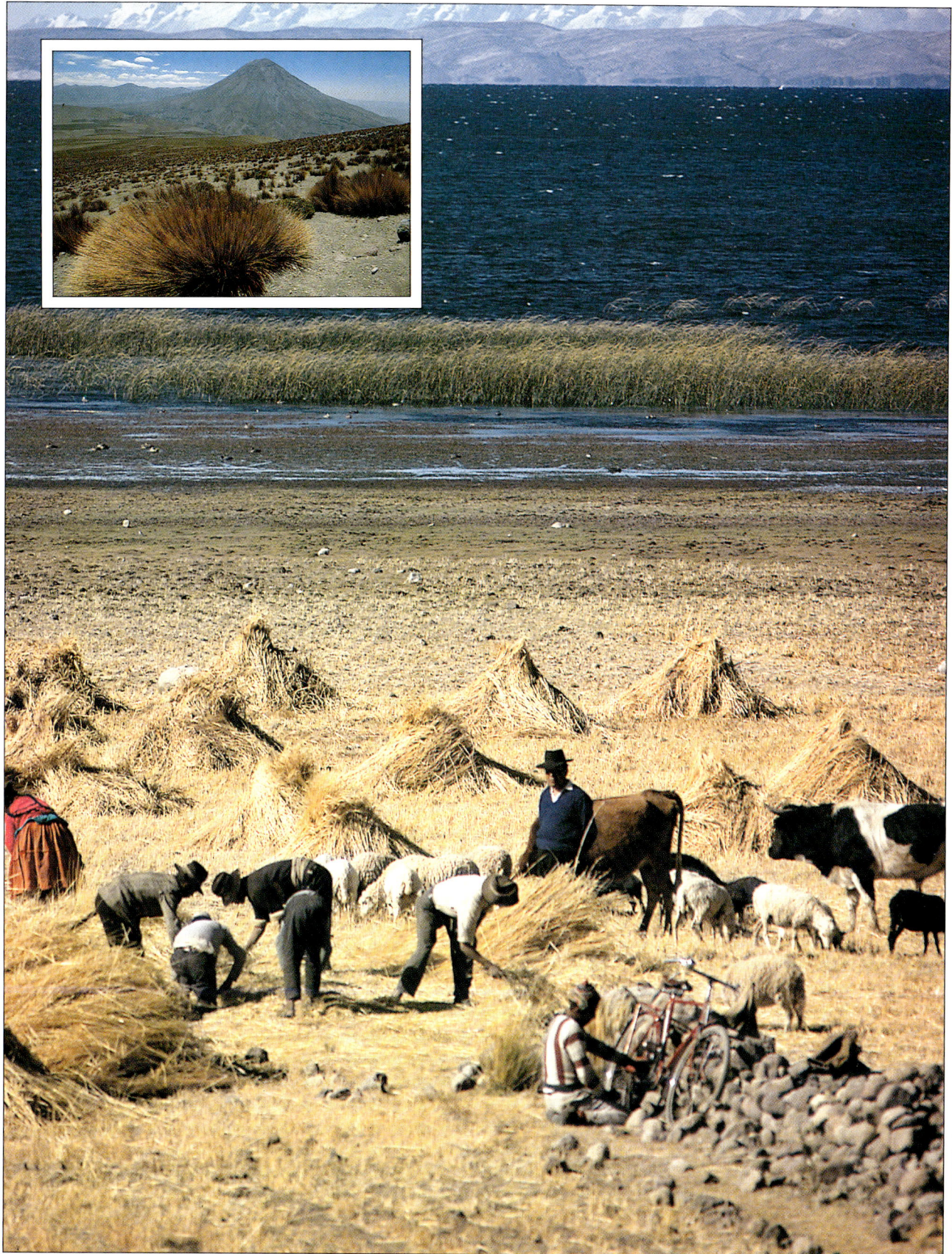

**View across Lake Titicaca eastward from Peru toward Bolivia**. This photograph was taken at the time of the barley harvest. It also shows some of the animals kept in this area.

The inset photograph shows the bleak scenery round the volcano El Misti in Peru. Only the very tough ichu grass will grow here.

# FARMERS

**The main way of life for most people living in the mountains is farming. In only a few places in the richest countries, such as Switzerland, has farming been replaced by the tourist industry.**

In some tropical and sub-tropical mountain lands farming is so successful that food is produced for the lowland peoples as well as for the mountain farmers themselves. For example, in the part of Nepal shown in the small photograph on the cover, enough rice is produced to sell some to the peoples of the lowlands. In contrast Nepalese farming, shown in the photograph on page 25, produces barely enough to feed the farmers and their families.

Another example of a mountainous area that can produce a food surplus is shown in the photograph on the left below. Here the rich volcanic mountain soils are being developed as quickly as possible. The demand for grapes and wines is growing rapidly as the tourist industry of Lanzarote develops.

Most mountain lands do not have the advantages of rich volcanic soils and a profitable tourist industry nearby. Many mountain peoples have a very low standard of living.

In some of the more prosperous mountain countries, like New Zealand and Norway, the mountains are used for farming in a rather different way. **The highland is used with the lowland.** For example, the photograph on page 29 of Naeroydalen Valley, Norway, shows a high summer pasture (saeter) which produces hay in the summer months. Much of the hay is taken down to the lowland to feed cattle there in the winter. Very few

**Making a vineyard on Lanzarote, Canary Islands.** The rich volcanic soils on the mountain side have been divided up into small round enclosures. This will reduce soil erosion, give shelter to new young vines and reduce water loss.

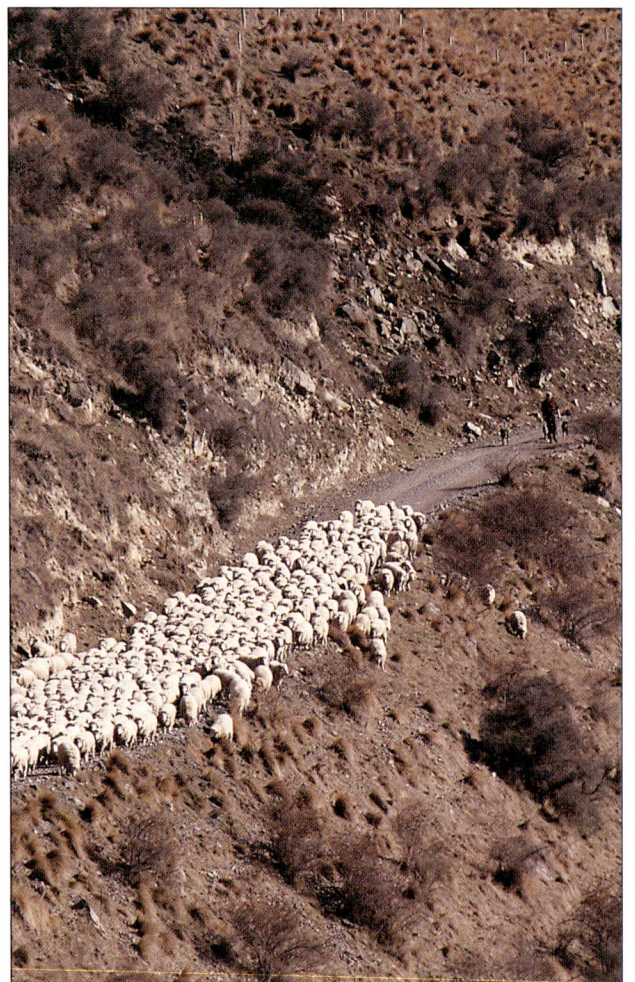

**Sheep round-up in the Rakia Gorge, South Island, New Zealand.**

**High altitude farmland in the Naeroydalen Valley, Stalheim, Norway.** The important crop here is hay for cattle. In Europe many small patches of mountain land like this are farmed only in the summer. Farm buildings may also be rented out to climbers and walkers. The people and animals return to the valleys in the winter. (Note how the clouds are forming over the high ground. The white mountain is not a volcano.)

animals remain on the high ground throughout the year. Because this pasture is linked with lowland farming it is also linked with the greater prosperity of the lowland. On slopes which are not too steep the hay fields can be worked by tractor instead of by hand as they are in poorer countries.

The photograph of the sheep round-up in New Zealand shows another example of this link between highland and lowland. The sheep are rounded up on the mountains in late summer and brought down to the lowland for the autumn sales. Those not sold must be kept throughout the winter in the warmer more sheltered lowlands.

**Key words**

**food surplus** – the amount of food left over for sale after all local needs have been met. A surplus is uncommon in most mountain lands.

**saeter** – Norwegian name for a clearing in the mountains.

**tourist industry** – all the kinds of work and workers involved in looking after visitors who do not stay long. Examples might include waiter, mountain guide and ski instructor.

# CHAPTER FIVE

# MOUNTAIN RESOURCES

## ROCKS AND WATER

In many mountain ranges the rocks have been intensely folded and changed by heat and pressure. (See chapter 2.) This has had two effects that interest miners:

1 Some rocks have been changed completely by the effects of heat and pressure. Two of the best known examples are:
   a) shales and mudstones are changed into **slate**,
   b) limestones are changed into **marble**. (See the photograph on page 31.)
2 Some rocks contain minerals which have been concentrated in particular places. Examples include gold, lead and copper.

These resources have led to many different kinds of mining. But in most cases the mines last only a short time as the metal is soon dug out. Not only are the mountain lands **exploited** by the miners almost nothing is done to **restore** the landscape afterwards.

The local people gained little long-term employment or any other benefit from the arrival of the miners. All they are left with today are exhausted mine workings and sometimes an abandoned ghost town.

In some ways the development of water resources in the mountains is also **exploitation**. The water may be stored in reservoirs for drinking or for the production of hydro-electric power (HEP). Once again the local people may receive little benefit from this. The water and the electricity are usually sent out of the mountains to the cities in the lowlands.

The flooding of mountain valleys can improve the scenery and encourage more visitors to come for **recreation**. But this may not make up for the loss of whole villages drowned behind the dams. Also lost is the better quality farmland and woodland on the lower slopes. A way of life has been changed for ever.

### HYDRO-ELECTRIC POWER STATION

Water from the dammed lake is piped down into the turbine house. The force of the water turns the turbines and this produces the electricity. The electricity is sent by power lines to the towns in the lowland.
The used water is sent down the valley either in the river or in a pipe to a lower reservoir.
When demand for electricity in the towns is low, for example, at night, the electricity being produced is used to pump water back uphill from the lower reservoir to the upper one. The water can be used over and over again. This means that quite a small lake can produce a lot of HEP.

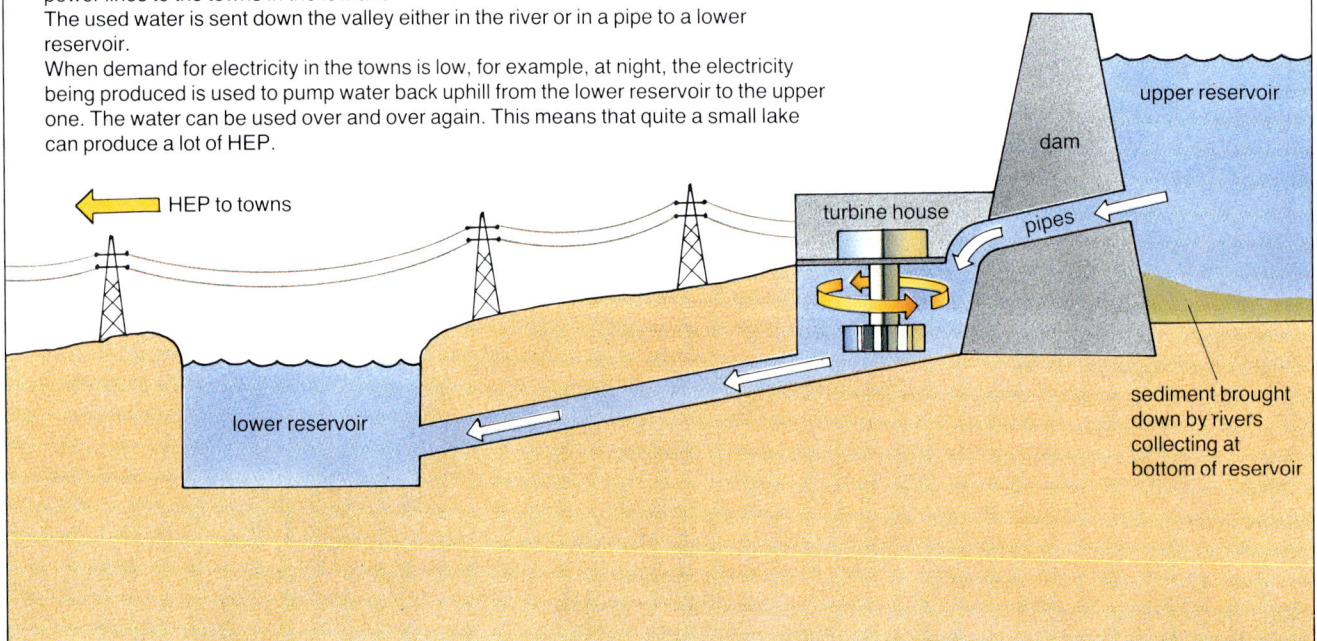

HEP to towns

lower reservoir

turbine house

pipes

dam

upper reservoir

sediment brought down by rivers collecting at bottom of reservoir

**Lac du Moiry dam and reservoir, Switzerland.** This beautiful lake has been formed by damming a mountain valley at a narrow point. The formation of this lake has drowned a mountain valley, cut communications and changed the environment completely. The pale blue colour of the lake is due to sediments carried into it by glacier and snow meltwater. Beyond the lake can be seen part of the Swiss Alps.

**A mountain marble quarry, near Salzburg, Austria.** Large blocks of marble are being cut with a continuous wire saw.

**Key words**

**exploitation** – taking a resource from an area without putting anything back.
**recreation** – play and relaxation. For example, at a reservoir recreation could include fishing, water-skiing and swimming.
**restore** – return a landscape to its original condition. For example, rubble and waste rock can be bulldozed back into an old mine working. Then topsoil can be replaced and trees planted.

# TREES

**In all the mountain lands trees are very important because they protect the environment.** They are a vital protection against soil erosion. Their roots bind the soil and their branches reduce the damaging effects of heavy rain storms. They slow down the speed of water running down and off the mountains. In this way they help prevent flooding on the lower lands. (See the diagram on page 33.)

Trees improve the environment in other ways as well. They add their leaves to the soil and enrich it. They also provide homes for the many birds, animals and insects in the environment.

When trees are cut down it is important to replace them at once with new young trees. In some of the the richer countries with big timber industries this is done by planting out young trees from tree nurseries. But in other places this is not done at all. (See the photograph below.) Because of greed or poverty and ignorance, the mountain slopes have been left bare. **The land is deforested.** As a result the most terrible damage is done by soil erosion.

The top soil is torn away by rain and melting snow and then carried down into the valleys. The mountains are left bare of any soil. There is no longer any possibility of quickly replacing the trees or of terracing the slopes for farming. The combination of steep slopes and high rainfall has destroyed the unprotected land.

In the valleys and plains below the mountains the rivers are choked with soil. They frequently overflow the surrounding country doing more damage. Lowland reservoirs and irrigation schemes are choked to death by all the sediment brought down by the rivers.

**Deforestation in Nepal.** The removal of the trees has led to severe soil erosion here. Land that might have been terraced for crops or used for new trees is now bare and useless.

## MAJOR DIFFERENCES BETWEEN FORESTED AND DEFORESTED SLOPES

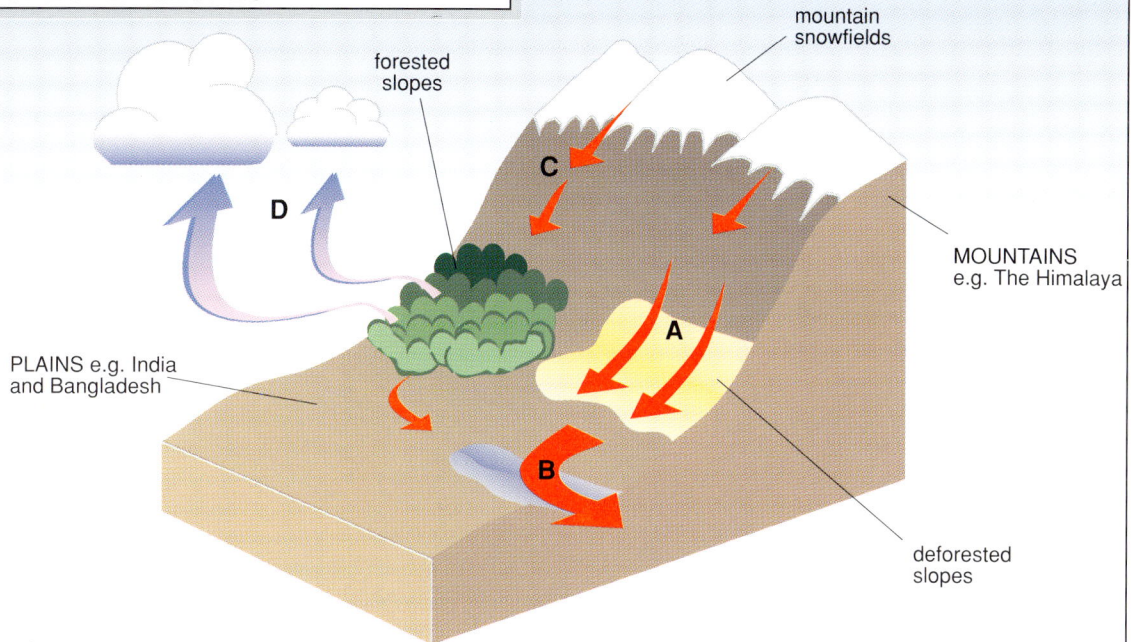

forested slopes

mountain snowfields

C

D

MOUNTAINS
e.g. The Himalaya

A

PLAINS e.g. India
and Bangladesh

B

deforested slopes

**Deforested slopes**

**A** Floodwaters (rain and snowmelt) cross deforested areas. The water is not retained by a forest cover. Soils are quickly eroded and carried down into the lowlands.

**B** Rivers choked with sediments burst their banks destroying farmlands and homes.

**Forested slopes**

**C** Rain and snowmelt retained or slowed down by forest cover.

**D** Much water evaporated into the air. Clouds take rain to dry areas or return it to the mountains.

The mountains and the plains are being destroyed together.

The worst example is in the Himalaya and the plain of the River Ganges to the south. (See the diagram above.) Experts believe that at the present rate of tree felling the Himalaya will be without trees and soils by the year 2015. At the same time, because water is no longer being held on the land by the trees, the lower ground will have become an arid drought-damaged region.

One country that shows some of the worst effects of deforestation is Nepal. The population will double to 30 millions by the year 2000. One result of this is that forest clearance has already increased to 120 000 hectares (296 520 acres) every year, **but only 15 000 hectares (37 065 acres) are replanted.** Most of the trees are used for firewood. Some of the cleared land is used for crops and animals but most of it is quickly destroyed by erosion.

Meanwhile in Bangladesh, a low-lying country on the Ganges delta, the number of serious floods increases every year. Here, in one of the world's poorest countries, people are being drowned and croplands destroyed. One of the causes of this is that trees are being cut down far away in other countries.

**Deforestation in Queenstown, Tasmania.**
Less than 100 years ago it was an important area for copper mining. Almost all the trees were cut down for fuel. As a result the soils were stripped off by erosion. The photograph shows how few plants have regrown in the last 80 years.

## TOURISM

**In many mountain lands the most valuable resource is the scenery.** The beauty of mountains plus the opportunity they give for many kinds of sports attracts large numbers of tourists. Even in very remote and isolated mountain lands the numbers of visitors are increasing. In the more accessible lands such as Switzerland the tourists provide a major source of income.

Tourists can be divided into two quite different groups:
1 spectators   2 sports people.

### 1 Spectators

These are the people who come to relax and look at the scenery. They are largely dependant on coach and car travel. They usually stay in comfortable hotels in the larger towns and villages in the mountain valleys. Spectators are interested in scenery that is accessible and does not require much effort to be enjoyed.

Most spectator tourists are summer rather than winter visitors to the mountains. They provide a huge income for the popular tourist resorts. But most of that income has to be earned in only three to four months of the summer. Most of these tourists are found in the wealthier mountain countries such as Switzerland, Austria, the USA and Canada. Few of these tourists would consider visiting the Himalaya in Asia or the Andes in South America. Those who do so want modern hotels to stay in and good roads to drive on.

**Tourist café overlooking the Mer de Glacé Glacier, France.** Tourists are carried up to this viewpoint by a cog and rack railway.

**A view in Milford Sound, New Zealand from a tour ship.** Viewing mountains from luxury tour ships is a popular holiday in Norway, in South Island, New Zealand and on the Pacific coasts of Canada and Alaska.

**Mountain view toward Patal Hiunchuli (6336 metres 20 788 feet) in the Himalaya, Nepal.** The number of tourists who enjoy this view is probably a few thousand each year. This compares with more than 12 million summer visitors to the Swiss Alps in Europe every year.

## 2 Sports People

This group of tourists includes people interested in a very wide range of activities. What they have in common is the aim to enjoy mountain scenery while being energetic. Sports people include hikers, campers, fishermen, mountaineers, skiers and tobogganists. Skiers may not regard fishermen as energetic but fishermen are prepared to climb up to good fishing lakes and streams, and not have their holiday organized round an hotel and a car.

Some of these tourists are prepared to go into more isolated parts of the mountain lands. Hill walkers and climbers want to extend their experience beyond the Swiss Alps to the Himalaya. Others wish to test their skills on peaks in Africa and South America. Their numbers are not very great but they often act rather like scouts for other tourists by opening up areas for the first time. Some of the national parks in Great Britain were first visited by mountaineers looking for new climbs. Today, these parks offer a full range of holiday activities.

Winter sports visitors are rather different from hikers and climbers. They require special and often expensive facilities such as chair lifts, ski runs, ice rinks and toboggan runs. In some mountain resorts the number of winter visitors is now greater than those who come in summer.

For people who live in the mountains winter sports visitors may be especially welcome. There are two special reasons for this:

1 These visitors come at a time when some other types of work have stopped for the winter. This includes quite a lot of farming work. Jobs in hotels, on the ski runs and at the ice rinks are available when some local people are unemployed.

2 Winter sports people are high-spending tourists. They not only pay for all the hotel facilities they need but also spend a lot of money on special equipment and facilities for their winter sports.

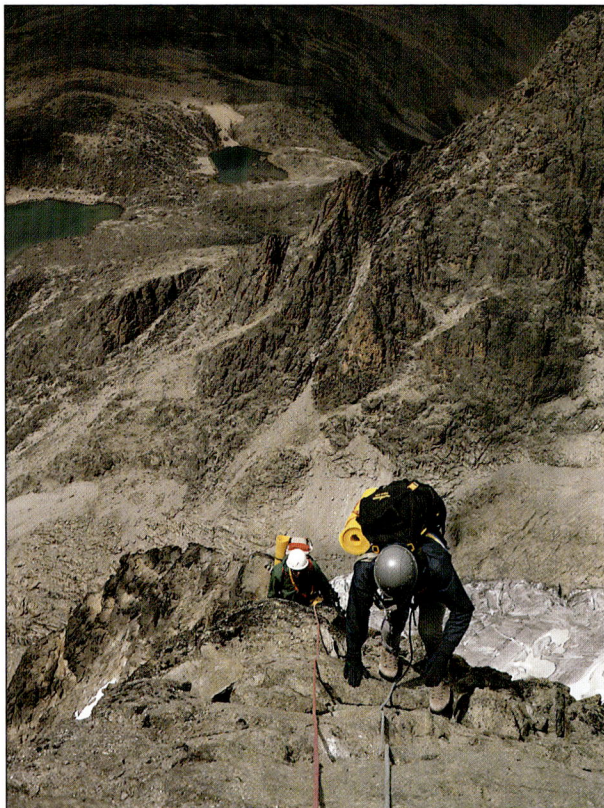

**Climbers approaching the summit of Mount Kenya in Africa.** This photograph was taken on the south-west ridge at about 5000 metres (16 405 feet).

**Skiing in the Selkirk Mountains, Canada at 2500 metres (8202 feet).**

**The Matterhorn, Zermatt, Switzerland.** This is the most famous and most visited mountain in the Alps. It draws both mountaineers and spectators to the area. The summit at 4477 metres (14 690 feet) bears a large banner cloud. The local weather at the top of the mountain is often very different from that at the bottom.

# CHAPTER SIX

# CONSERVATION IN THE MOUNTAINS

**Conservation is the protection of an environment and its resources from exploitation.**

The protection of mountain lands has become very important. Programmes of conservation are being drawn up and used in several mountain lands. There are three main groups of reasons why conservation is needed in the mountains.

1 **Mountain environments are fragile.**

Some of the reasons why this is so have already been described. They include:

a) Mountain slopes are always in danger from erosion.

b) Unreliable and often bad weather can be destructive of plant, animal and human life. Some areas are also affected by volcanic activity and earthquakes.

c) Many mountain lands are poor environments for people to live in. The weather is often bitterly cold, summer is short, soils are poor and crops are small.

d) Mountain people often lack the education and money to look after their environment themselves.

2 **Mountain environments are now in danger from overpopulation.**

Overpopulation means that the numbers of people (or animals) living in an area is too many for that area to support. For example, this is beginning to happen in the mountain lands of Bolivia, Peru and Nepal.

Because mountain environments are fragile, overpopulation can happen very quickly. For example, if the population of

**Logan Pass in the Glacier National Park, Montana, USA.** There are nearly 100 national parks in North America. Many of them, like the Glacier National Park, include large areas of mountain land. The duckboards seen in the foreground of this photograph make walking easier but also help to reduce erosion of the plant cover on busy footpaths.

a remote mountain village in Nepal **doubles** from 100 to 200 people that may be a disaster. But in a lowland village, with much good farmland, the population might increase tenfold from 100 to 1000 before there was any real shortage of food. Also the skills and money needed for better water supplies, roads and hospitals are more often available in the lowlands than in remote mountain ranges.

3 **Some mountain environments are in danger from over-use.**

The worst example of this over-use of mountains is found in some of the mountain tourist areas of the richer countries such as Switzerland and Austria. Mountain environments are simply being worn out. In some places mountain tracks have been so trampled down all the plant life is dead. Footpaths have to be protected from the feet of walkers. (See the photograph on page 38.)

In other places the success of tourism has attracted farmers and foresters away from their old jobs and into the hotel business. The result is that the mountain landscape is no longer being properly looked after.

**Conservation does not mean that all these developments must stop.** (It is far too late for that anyway.) Conservation means that developments will be much more carefully controlled to protect the mountain lands from over-use. If this succeeds there will still be some groups of mountain peoples living in mountain communities in the 21st century. There will also be some mountain environments left for all of us to enjoy.

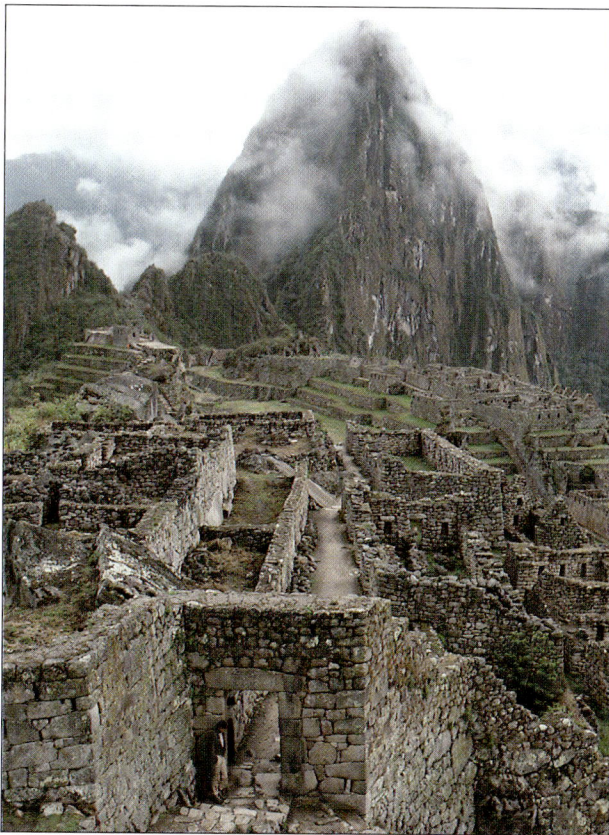

**Machu Picchu was a great city built by the ancient Inca civilization at an altitude of 2400 metres (7874 feet) in the Andes of Peru.** At the moment only small numbers of tourists visit this high altitude site, but as communications are improved more visitors will come here. A conservation programme must be set up **before** that happens.

**Cable car descending from Schilthorn to Mürren, Switzerland.** Cable cars carry many tourists up to the higher areas of mountain lands.

**An avalanche at 7000 metres (22 967 feet) on Annapurna II in the Himalaya.** A collapsing ice cliff has started the movement of the snows below it. Most avalanches occur in the spring as the land begins to be warmed and the snow and ice begin to thaw. Areas of unstable snow, like that shown in the photograph on the title page, often trigger avalanches.

Development of the mountain lands has to be through programmes of conservation. These programmes will attempt to put right the mistakes of the past. They will also have to prevent those mistakes being made again.

The most important example is reforesting the mountains. More damage has been done in the mountains by cutting down trees than by anything else. Soil erosion is destroying every part of the mountain way of life. In the mountains, wood is wealth in several ways. A properly organized forestry industry with a replanting programme gives the people a long-lasting source of work and income. Much more important it reduces soil erosion. A wooded slope holds back rain and snow meltwater far better than the surfaces of car parks, ski runs, roads and buildings.

The replanting of forests also helps reduce damage by avalanches. Avalanches cannot be entirely prevented but they can be slowed down by trees. Many Swiss and Austrian alpine villages have shelter belts of trees above and around them. They give some protection against the impact of an avalanche.

One of the situations that encourages avalanches is a bare smooth, frozen slope. Unfortunately, this is quite a good description of a ski slope. In some winter sports centres the number of ski slopes is being reduced by replanting with trees.

Tourism is a major area where the local people need to take control of what is happening in their homeland. All too often it has been the people from outside the mountain lands who have controlled matters. It has been their decisions to build more hotels, roads or second homes for the rich. The local way of life has been overwhelmed. Worse still, when a tourist centre has been completely overdeveloped, the tourists have often decided they do not like it any more. They have moved on to a new centre until that too is spoiled.

In some Swiss mountain valleys all the farmhouses have become hotels. Very few people now work full time on the land. Woodlands are not cared for, pastures are becoming eroded and drainage ditches are blocked. All the ways in which farmers and foresters look after the environment are being neglected.

**The Europa Bridge on the main autobahn from Austria through the Brenner Pass to Italy.**

In a few cases the local people are beginning to take action to restrict this over-development. The Swiss resort of Grindlewald has about a million visitors a year and many rich Swiss have built second homes there. A new development plan has been drawn up by the local people. A first step was to control the development of the cable car system. The old cable cars were to be replaced by very large new ones named gondolas. Gondolas can hold 1600 people! The local council has stopped this and restricted the size to 1200 people. For the cable car company the profits will be less. But for the town it will mean fewer new car parks and fewer new ski runs on the mountain slopes.

**In some mountain lands the people cannot do very much themselves. They need international help to conserve their mountains.** For example, the people of Nepal cannot afford to start the huge programme of tree planting that is needed there. They have to replant 170 000 hectares (420 070 acres) of trees every year just to stop the situation getting any worse. At the moment thay cannot manage 10 per cent of that replanting. (See page 33.)

There is another reason why international

action is needed. Much of the damage being done in the mountains is caused by events outside the mountain lands.

One example is that mountain trees are being severely damaged by pollution. The main cause is traffic fumes, and one of the worst places is shown in the photograph above. This superb road is the main Common Market route to the south through Austria. It is used by 10 million cars a year and 5000 trucks a day. The huge quantities of exhaust gases, especially the nitrogen oxides, are rapidly killing off the trees over distances of many kilometres. Another disadvantage is that, although it was constructed as a through route, this road is also attracting more local traffic via the slip roads that lead to it.

In other mountain areas the forests and lakes are being destroyed by acid rain. The rain washes down the chemicals in the air that have drifted in from other countries. Much of the damage caused by acid rain in Norway and Sweden is the result of pollution from British power stations which has been blown across the North Sea. Problems like these can only be dealt with by international co-operation.

# CONCLUSIONS

**Everywhere the mountain lands are in a state of crisis. Crisis means danger and opportunity. The danger is that we continue to exploit the mountain lands in the same harmful ways as in the past. The opportunity is that we recognize the damage being done and change our behaviour.**

The first change is that we accept it costs a lot of money to protect mountain environments (and any other environments). Part of the cost of developing a mountain resource is the cost of repairing the damage. For example, we can make sure that the costs of mining include the costs of restoring the landscape afterwards.

When a government grants mining rights restoring the land must be included in the agreement. When mining ends the workings can be landscaped and planted with trees. If the company fails to carry out the agreement then it can be taken to court and fined the huge sums of money necessary to pay for restoring the land. (It is true that old mine workings do attract tourists but we have plenty of these already.)

A second example of developing and conserving the environment is the National Parks that have been set up in most countries. Many of these parks protect large areas of mountain country. But many of them have become a victim of their own success.

In the last 35 years there has been an explosion of wealth in most western countries, and also in others like Japan, Australia and New Zealand. Many more families have cars, caravans, boats and other kinds of sports gear. Millions of people now visit the parks.

The most popular parks suffer problems of over-use including soil erosion, pollution, litter and other kinds of environmental damage. We have to face the costs of repair. One way of dealing with this is to put environmental taxes on every service provided by the parks. Everything will have to be more expensive to pay for the upkeep of the parks. It has also become necessary to close off some park areas while paths are reseeded, lakes cleaned and pollution damage repaired.

However hard we work to develop mountain areas in ways that do not damage the environment that will not be enough. **We have to recognize that the mountains are being affected by worldwide problems as well as local problems. Two of the worldwide problems are pollution and overpopulation.**

The problem of pollution has been discussed on pages 40 and 41. Until we stop burning fuels, petrols and oils without proper environmental controls every new tree we plant in the mountains is likely to be damaged. The reason why this is especially serious in mountain environments is that trees play a vital role there in restricting soil erosion on steep slopes.

Few people live in the mountains yet many mountain areas now suffer from overpopulation. In many places the problem is made worse because the people who are overpopulating the mountains are also very poor. Even if they understand birth control and have no religious objections to using it they still have large families.

In these poor communities the only way old people are looked after is by their children. So a family of fourteen children is a better investment for the parents than a family of two children. As a result there is more and more pressure on the mountain lands to feed more people, and to supply more fuel and building materials. Until proper welfare schemes are shown to be working in these lands couples will have large families. This may mean that people will have to be paid for not having children, just as mountain farmers might be paid for not running hotels but staying on the land.

**The Royal Valley of the Incas, with the town of Urubamba and the Andes Mountains, Peru.** At the frontiers between town and country, mountain and lowland there is much to be learned. The mountain lands share in the problems of the lowlands as well as having problems of their own. But because mountain environments are in a state of delicate balance they can change very quickly into a state of crisis. **We are learning a lot about conservation and exploitation in the mountains.**

# GLOSSARY

**adapted** – a plant or animal that has changed so that is can survive in a different environment.

**conservation** – the protection of an environment and its resources from exploitation.

**Continental Drift** – the very slow movement of continents as they are carried on the underlying plates.

**crisis** – a time of change, a time of danger and opportunity.

**environment** – what a place is like and how the people live in it.

**erosion** – the breakdown and removal of rocks.

**exploitation** – taking from an environment without putting anything back.

**facilities** – equipment and special places for tourists, for example: ice skates and an ice rink.

**fault** – a break in the rocks.

**fold** – a bend in the rocks.

**magma** – hot molten rock in the interior of the Earth.

**precipitation** – all the forms in which water falls to the ground.

**recreation** – play and relaxation, for example: rock climbing and fishing.

**restore** – return a landscape to its original condition.

**saeter** – Norwegian name for a clearing in the mountains. In Switzerland a saeter is named an alp – hence the name of the mountains, The Alps.

**sedimentary** – rocks laid down in layers of sediment, usually in water.

**tourist** – a paying visitor who comes to enjoy a place but who does not stay long.

**volcanic activity** – the escape of magma, gases and steam to the Earth's surface.

# FURTHER READING

## INTRODUCTORY BOOKS

Dixon, D. *Mountians: Franklin Watts Picture Atlas* Franklin Watts 1984
Lye, K. *Our World: Mountains* Wayland 1986
Morrison, M. *Indians of the Andes* Wayland 1985
Williams, L. *The Changing Earth* (series) Ginn 1984
Especially:
*Highlands and Lowlands*
*Volcanoes and Earthquakes*

## MORE ADVANCED READING

Bain, I. *Mountains and Earth Movements* Wayland 1984
Cameron, I. *Exploring the Himalayas* Longman 1985

Clark, R.W. *Men, Myth and Mountains* Weidenfeld & Nicholson 1976
Newby, E. *Great Ascents* David and Charles 1977
Perry, M. *Mountain Wildlife* Croom Helm 1981
Robin, G. *Glaciers and Ice Sheets* Wayland 1984
Time Life (series) *Volcanoes* Time Life Books Inc. 1982
Williams, L. and Collinson, A. *Last Frontiers for Mankind* (series) Evans Brothers Limited 1990
Especially:
*Understanding the Polar Lands*
*Conserving the Jungles*
*Working with the Oceans*